THOSE FABULOUS MOVIE YEARS:

THE 30s

by PAUL TRENT

BARRE PUBLISHING

BARRE, MASSACHUSETTS

Distributed by CROWN PUBLISHERS, INC. NEW YORK

A Vineyard Book

ACKNOWLEDGMENTS

For their help and encouragement in the preparation of this book, the author is deeply grateful to: George Malko, Regina Grant Hersey, Peter Dworkin, Joan Crawford, Ruth Creasap, Jack Neal, Miriam Shinnick, Helen Killeen, Lou Valentino, Betty Hill, Lou Gross, Viola Fafangel, Saul Jaffe, Susan Schulman, Max Rosenthal and the studios—20th Century–Fox Film Corporation, Metro-Goldwyn-Mayer, Inc., Universal, United Artists, Selznick International, Samuel Goldwyn Productions and RKO-Radio Pictures.

An original work created and produced by
VINEYARD BOOKS, INC.
  159 East 64th Street
  New York, N. Y. 10021

Copyright © 1975 by Vineyard Books, Inc.
Library of Congress Catalogue Card Number: 75–4174
ISBN: 0-517-512407

Manufactured in the United States of America

Trent, Paul, 1940-
    The 30s.

    (Those fabulous movie years)
    1. Moving-pictures--United States--History. I. Title. II. Series.
PN1993.5.U6T72   791.43'0973   75-4174
ISBN 0-517-51240-7

CONTENTS

Marlene Dietrich poses against the posh backdrop of her living room

THE 30s

On November 13, 1929, following three shattering weeks that had witnessed a panic-ridden collapse of stock-market prices, Wall Street hit its low for the year. In the brief rally that followed, the financial masterminds, headed by President Herbert Hoover, emerged from their sanctuaries to offer words of good cheer to the stricken multitude. Bankers, industrialists, economic forecasters all said substantially the same thing: Conditions were basically sound. The ''lunatic'' fringe of speculators had been driven out of the marketplace, and prices could now rise on a ''sound'' foundation. Good times were just around the corner.

No voice was raised to predict that two years later those November lows would tower like Mt. Everest above the depths to which securities would eventually drop. Or that by 1932 one out of every four workers would be jobless—somewhere between thirteen and fifteen million individuals. Or that the longest, deepest and

4

most devastating depression of modern times would linger on until nearly the end of the decade.

That same period was a traumatic time as well for one of the few industries that prospered during the 30s—motion pictures. Several years earlier enlightened tinkerers had perfected the technique of synchronizing pictures and words on the screen. When, in 1927, Al Jolson appeared in the first all-talking picture—*The Jazz Singer*—the movie-making centers of the world turned topsy-turvy overnight. Some silent films were abandoned outright, some were patched up with sound effects and some were released, only to discover that theaters throughout the nation had been converted to sound and showed not the least desire to exhibit relics of a bygone age.

As the 30s dawned, dozens of top stars with shrill, squeaky, effeminate or coarse voices suddenly found their careers at an end. In their stead each week saw trains like the Chief and the Super Chief rumble into their Los Angeles terminus bearing recruits from the legitimate or vaudeville stage. Some were already big names, such as Fredric March, who had considerable trouble adapting to sound; his early efforts sounded arch and stilted. Others, like Gable and Bogart, Cagney and Lombard were among the unknowns destined to become the Barthelmesses and Fairbankses, the John Gilberts or the Janet Gaynors of the new era.

Many of the silent stars made an easy transition to talking pictures: Joan Crawford, Norma Shearer, Greta Garbo, Gary Cooper and Ronald Colman grew enormously in stature. Marion Davies escaped papier-mâché backgrounds and proved that she was a good comedian. Some stars who had been in relative obscurity for years—Marie Dressler and Wallace Beery are two good examples— soared to the top. And some, like Ramon Novarro, hung on in roles that progressively grew smaller and smaller.

If it had not been for the movies, the 30s would have been an even sorrier time for the average American. For from 10 to 50 cents you could see a double feature, plus a cartoon, plus a newsreel, plus (at the top price) an hour-long stage show headed by top talent—up to five or more hours in which to forget the endless waiting in long lines for jobs that didn't exist, the ominous letters from the electric company, the gas company, the phone company, the landlord, all saying the same thing: pay up . . . or else.

What is there one can say in disparagement of the films of the 30s? Well, first of all, they were ground out in an assembly-line fashion. Big stars appeared in four or more films a year; successful character actors often quadrupled that number. Secondly, beginning in 1933, studios suffered from pressure groups—church and civic organizations combined with a Hollywood "code" that made Queen Victoria look like a brazen hussy. A husband and wife could not be shown together in bed. A kiss was restricted in length and performed with tightly clamped lips. The precise manner in which a male body encountered a female structure was regulated in detail. Gangsters and Western badmen could say "shucks" or "golly," but a line like "the hell with it" was way out of bounds. It wasn't until 1939 that a shocked public heard Rhett Butler say "I don't give a damn" as he left Scarlett O'Hara for the last time. Only Gable could have gotten away with a line like that.

While in theory the movie-makers were producing Puritan films for a Puritanical

Humphrey Bogart dressing for a gala—a view of Bogie never seen on screen

Hollywood style setters of the 30s—a white-tied Maurice Chevalier, a tuxedoed Marlene Dietrich and Gary Cooper in the latest wide-lapel fashion

public, considerable s-e-x crept into a lot of them. Writers inserted *double-entendres* into their scripts. While nudity was of course banned, female stars, with Harlow setting the pace, discarded all undergarments and appeared on screen in the filmiest and most revealing fabrics being produced. It is indeed alleged that she placed ice on her nipples just before going on camera. Some have speculated that part of the enormous appeal of the Tarzan films stemmed from their semi-nudity. Johnny Weissmuller cavorted about with his generative area protected by something resembling a bib attached to a G-string, while Maureen O'Sullivan wore a skillfully designed jungle bra and mini-miniskirt.

Whatever criticisms one may make of the films of the 30s, the fact remains that the decade produced a bountiful crop of truly fine motion pictures. With few exceptions, notably King Vidor's *Our Daily Bread*, 1934, the Depression as a central theme was ignored. Escapism was the order of the day, and film-makers transported audiences to Shangri-La and the jungles of deepest Africa, to the drawing rooms of the very rich and the perils of the old West, to the burning of

6

Atlanta and gangster hangouts, to the Land of Oz and the home of Dopey, Grumpy, Sneezy and their four companions.

One outstanding feature of the decade was the speed with which directors and cameramen mastered the new technology of sound films. The art of special effects soared to a new peak in films like *Frankenstein*, 1931, *King Kong*, 1933, *The Invisible Man*, 1933, and *The Hurricane*, 1937. In dozens of overblown musicals directors like Busby Berkeley used startling new camera angles to depict squadrons of dancers and singers performing with a military precision that put West Point cadets to shame—a new art form that culminated with perhaps the lushest film of them all, *The Great Ziegfeld*, 1936.

Film-making in the 30s was by no means confined to Hollywood. German studios, which made significant contributions to films in the 20s, diminished in importance after Goebbels took them over as part of Hitler's propaganda machine. *M*, with Peter Lorre in 1931, and *Maedchen in Uniform* in 1932 were the last impressive German efforts. Mussolini's Italy was equally unproductive, while the Scandinavian countries were just beginning to make their presence felt with films like *Swedenhielms*, 1935, with Ingrid Bergman. France, with brilliant directors like René Clair, turned out such beauties as *Sous les Toits de Paris* (*Under the Roofs of Paris*), 1931. Particularly stunning was *La Kermesse Héroïque* (*Carnival in Flanders*), 1936, a sly Gallic farce whose underlying sexiness somehow eluded the censors.

England, with Gaumont-British and other new studios, was coming up fast. The 30s saw the arrival on the scene of Alfred Hitchcock, who in his native land directed three of the best thrillers ever—*The Man Who Knew Too Much*, 1935, *The 39 Steps*, 1935, and *The Lady Vanishes*, 1938. (What true film buff can ever forget Miss Froy?)

Although many British actors, like Ronald Colman, had fled to the gold mines of Hollywood, there were other fine English-made films as well. René Clair came from Paris to star Robert Donat in *The Ghost Goes West*, 1935. Alexander Korda made history with *The Private Life of Henry VIII*, 1933, as did Robert Flaherty with *Man of Aran*, 1934. *Pygmalion*, 1938, Gabriel Pascal's adaptation of the Shaw play, was another fine effort.

Basically, however, it was the huge Hollywood studios that ruled the movie roost. It was to that pre-smogbound Hollywood that German directors like Lubitsch and Von Sternberg fled, that actresses like Binnie Barnes and Charles Laughton (clutching the best-actor award he had won for *The Private Life of Henry VIII*) traveled. Almost always the move added luster and lucre to their careers. M-G-M, tightly in the clutches of Louis B. Mayer and managed by a brilliant and short-lived young man named Irving Thalberg, controlled the most stars, had the biggest budgets and made the slickest (and many of the best) films of the 30s. Paramount was a power, and Warner Brothers, under the shrewd leadership of Jack Warner, had a special touch with gangster films and smash-hit musicals. Columbia, run by an extremely tough gentleman named Harry Cohn, became a power in the movie colony after releasing *It Happened One Night* in 1934. It was Cohn's funeral, attended by thousands, that provoked a local wag to comment: "Give the public what they want and they'll turn out." RKO, after Fred Astaire and Ginger Rogers

Shedding her undergarments enabled Jean Harlow to show her fans all that the censors would permit.

danced the Carioca in *Flying Down to Rio* in 1933, grew mightily, while a fugitive from Warners, Darryl Zanuck, co-founded 20th Century in 1933 (the merger with Fox came in 1935) and soon made it another power in the Hollywood hierarchy.

The big stars, from Bette Davis and James Cagney down, waged endless warfare with studio tycoons—objecting, usually with good reason, to the films assigned them, battling over salaries, trying to escape typecasting. After attaining stardom George Raft objected to the role of Baby Face Martin in *Dead End*, 1937. Martin had no redeeming features whatsoever, and Raft wanted a speech inserted wherein he could tell the street gang that crime really didn't pay in the long run. The studio refused, and the part went to Humphrey Bogart, along with several others of a similar nature that Raft also refused to play. Even Shirley Temple got into the act. When Graham Greene wrote that maybe Shirley wasn't the all-time child genius (he really thought precious little of her capabilities), Greene was sued both by Shirley and her studio.

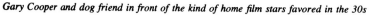

Gary Cooper and dog friend in front of the kind of home film stars favored in the 30s

Like most big stars, Joel McCrea selected the ultimate in motor transport.

The 30s saw the star system reach its peak. At a time when factory workers and white-collar employees were drawing salaries that ranged from $40 to less than half that amount a week, scores of starred players drew from $3,000 to $10,000 or more per week. Unlike the big stars of the 20s, they no longer spent their money building huge mausoleums like Pickfair on the fringes of Sunset Boulevard. Now the movement was away from Hollywood and a bit farther out—to Beverly Hills and Pacific Palisades or Coldwater Canyon. One- and two-story ranch houses, equipped, of course, with pool and tennis court, were coming into vogue, but the acreage was reduced, the lawns and gardens less lavish.

Back in the 20s the Fatty Arbuckle scandal, the tragic death of Mabel Normand, the drug-induced death of Wallace Reid, plus half a dozen other lurid episodes had convinced the public that life in Hollywood was one long round of orgies. In the 30s things had quieted down a lot. Intellectual life centered around the refugees from the East—playwrights and novelists, poets and short-story writers, almost all of whom counted the days before they could get back to New York. They mingled with writers like Billy Wilder and Charles Brackett, Ben Hecht and Charles MacArthur (who rather liked California) and with actors like Edward G. Robinson, who had begun to build a notable art collection. Some stars, like Miriam Hopkins and Constance Bennett, had clauses in their contracts that gave them time off each year for a stay in the East.

9

A day's fan mail for a delighted Joan Crawford. Whether or not she read all those letters remains a guarded secret.

Big parties were few and far between and for the most part were as boring as New Year's Eve spent dancing to the music of Guy Lombardo in the Grand Ballroom of the Waldorf-Astoria. Small home parties, roughly speaking, could be divided into two categories: first, those held by the thinking element in the movie colony—actors like Edward G. Robinson or Carole Lombard, directors and screenwriters like Billy Wilder or Charles Lederer, plus a host of Broadway playwrights and novelists who were serving time in Hollywood; second, parties at which the men congregated at one end of the living room to talk shop and the ladies at the other to discuss clothes and local gossip.

10

Then there were the goer-outers, whose every move was reported by Louella Parsons and for whom cameramen waited in droves. One danced at Ciro's or the Trocadero. One dined at the Brown Derby or La Rue. One dressed up and went to premieres. One went to the glossy hotels for fashion shows or benefits. When things got desperate Las Vegas or Tijuana or Palm Springs and the desert were havens of refuge.

Although an overwhelming percentage of Hollywood couples led quiet lives and even managed to stay married, enough happened to make headlines that evoked cluckings from the general public. The shenanigans (usually alcoholic) of John Barrymore and Errol Flynn are cases in point. There was even a shooting or two. In that early era Howard Hughes, before his recluse era, was photographed with a different starlet clinging to his arm almost every night.

It is true that the divorce and remarriage rate in Hollywood was far higher than in the rest of the nation. No doubt part of the reason stemmed from the fact that Hollywood contained more handsome men and sexy females than any other city in the world. There was another cause as well: the murderous work schedules. Shooting often began at dawn and lasted until nightfall. Often a movie husband and wife, working on different locations, wouldn't see each other for weeks on end. As they worked in an ever-rising atmosphere of pressure, it is not hard to understand the fate that overcame Jean Harlow and, later, Judy Garland and Marilyn Monroe. Or why actors and actresses married and married and married and married.

This, then, was Hollywood in the 30s. A town filled with beautiful and too often semiliterate men and women who suddenly found themselves famous. A town with uncounted thousands of call girls who commanded up to $1,000 a night. A town full of shrewd businessmen and brilliant directors and thoughtful art- and book-loving actors.

Hollywood was the nation's leader in bad taste. And, quite often, good taste as well. Its Art Deco palazzos were the best—and the worst—ever built. It was a town of phonies and of down-to-earth people, of seekers of the fast buck and of dedicated artists, of sleek limousines and of tattered jalopies, of sleazy one-room apartments climbing the steep slopes of Hollywood and of fabulous mansions. It was filled with dreamers of dreams of stardom that would never come true. In short, post-Depression Hollywood was utterly unlike any other sleepy town in the world that suddenly found itself a mini-metropolis. With the coming of the war years it retained some of its kookiness, but it was never again quite the way it was in the 30s.

ALBERT R. LEVENTHAL

11

Luise Rainer, the appealing Austrian star who won best-actress Oscars in 1935 and 1936

Richard Cromwell in title role

Tol'able David (1930)

During the early months of 1930 excitement and anticipation rose to feverish proportions at Columbia studios as director John Blystone tirelessly tested more than 200 juvenile actors for the starring role of David in his upcoming remake of the 1921 silent-film classic *Tol' able David*, which had starred Richard Barthelmess. Finally, in early April, at the insistence of his friends, a 20 year-old Los Angeles artist and gallery operator named Ray Radabough tried for the part. Director Blystone's enthusiastic response to the screen test was an immediate ''Sign him! But change his name.'' Thus, a new star, Richard Cromwell, was born.

Tol' able David was a combination of a loosely allegorical retelling of the Biblical David and Goliath story and the story of the famous feuding families, the Hatfields and the McCoys. David Kinemon's father is murdered and his brother crippled by Luke Hatburn, a member of the opposing clan. Of course, David must avenge these foul deeds and in the end confronts and defeats the giant of a man (played by Noah Beery).

Released in November 1930, the film was praised by critics, was successful at the box office and was effective as a vehicle for launching its star. Yet John Blystone's straightforward direction produced a film less momorable than director Henry King's vivid, heart-warming original. Richard Cromwell's performance, though fresh and appealing, lacked the persuasiveness and power of Richard Barthelmess' 1921 characterization. The additional dimension of sound is perhaps the film's most distinguishing characteristic when compared to the earlier version.

Joan Peers, Richard Cromwell and Noah Beery

Richard Cromwell and Joan Peers

Helen Ware and Richard Cromwell

All Quiet on the Western Front (1930)

Audiences and critics throughout the world have come to regard this film as one of the screen's most powerful antiwar documents. Adapted from Erich Maria Remarque's novel of World War I by Pulitzer Prize-winning playwright Maxwell Anderson (with assistance from George Abbott and Dell Andrews), the film packs emotional power and moral persuasiveness by juxtaposing the tranquillity of life in a small German town with the filth, horror and anguish of warfare.

Director Lewis Milestone skillfully alternates ultrarealistic battlefield footage with more studied scenes concentrating on human values and relationships. On these opposite dimensions of human experience he overlays with dramatic effect contrasts of sound—the noise of cannon fire and machine guns, followed by fearful silences—and visual images—as in the final scene, when Lew Ayres' hand reaches out for a butterfly and falls limp as a bullet rips through his body—to create a film of unique and timeless beauty.

Milestone's lyrical direction netted him his second Oscar (his first was for best comedy direction of *Two Arabian Nights* in 1927). Louis Wolheim, Ayres and silent comedian Raymond Griffith contributed fine performances in the lead roles and helped *All Quiet on the Western Front* win best-picture honors for 1930. No film has ever deserved it more.

Lewis Ayres and Louis Wolheim

Lewis Ayres as Paul Baumer

Lewis Ayres and Raymond Griffith

Gary Cooper as Tom Brown and Marlene Dietrich as Amy Jolly

Gary Cooper and Marlene Dietrich in the cabaret

Morocco (1930)

The principal attraction of *Morocco* for American audiences was their first glimpse of Josef von Sternberg's discovery and protégé, Marlene Dietrich. Though *The Blue Angel* was the actress-director team's first film together, the German-made work was not released in the United States until Dietrich had been promoted in an extensive publicity campaign and established as a star.

In both films she plays a cabaret performer, one in Berlin, the other on the fringes of the Moroccan desert. In *The Blue Angel* she is naughty Lola who drives lonely professor Emil Jannings to social disgrace and moral degradation. In *Morocco*, however, the tables are somewhat turned. Though she does spurn the love of Kennington (Adolphe Menjou) and breaks his heart, she does so because she finds herself irresistibly attracted to Tom Brown (Gary Cooper). Her sensuous Amy Jolly unsuccessfully contends with the cool, independent sex appeal of Legionnaire Cooper. His dark, long-lashed bedroom eyes easily best her come-hither, I'm-unconquerable posturing, and by the film's finale she has been reduced to his slave. She doffs her high heels and, with the other camp followers, staggers obediently after him and his regiment as the men go to fight a desert war.

Time has not been kind to *Morocco*; its tenets are intolerable to a culture dedicated to basic equality. But the film has a historic appeal, for it evinces all of Von Sternberg's distinctive touches: wearyingly slow pacing of action; preoccupation with interplay of light and shadow; careful attention to detail in costumes and sets; frequent filming through gauze, making the actors appear to be moving through liquid space; and the lingering impression one has entered a world less significant for its real values than for its plastic ones.

The film marked an auspicious beginning for Marlene Dietrich. She was nominated for an Academy Award for her performance. It was also Gary Cooper's best role until *Lives of a Bengal Lancer*, 1935.

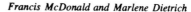

Francis McDonald and Marlene Dietrich

Adolphe Menjou, the spurned lover, with Marlene Dietrich

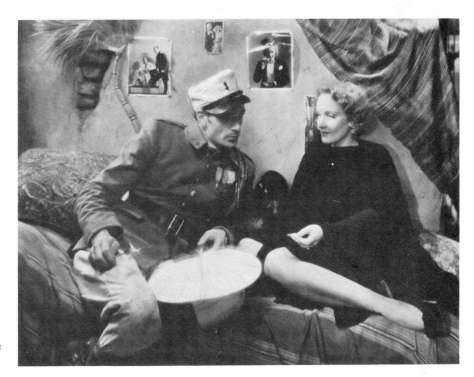

Gary Cooper and Marlene Dietrich

Production shot of final sequence

The Spoilers (1930)

Gary Cooper and William "Stage" Boyd starred in this third filming of Rex Beach's popular saga of Alaskan gold-mining. (The 1914 silent featured Tom Santschi and William Farnum; Milton Sills and Noah Beery played the roles in 1923.) The chief attractions in this superior rendition were Cooper's persuasive performance as the sympathetic but rugged Glenister and Edward Carewe's impressive, flexible camera work and expert pacing of the action and mounting suspense. Especially noteworthy as well was the vigorous, sweaty, climactic barroom slug-out between Cooper and Boyd which set the standard for authenticity in movie brawling for years to come.

The female parts, played by Kay Johnson and Betty Compson, were admirably done, but ultimately they only served to underscore that this was, as the saying goes, a man's movie. Even a stereotyped subplot of female jealousy—Cooper falls for Johnson's charms, sending Compson into a rage—focuses the action on Cooper, who outschemes and outsmarts the two schemers—or, rather, spoilers—a corrupt judge (Lloyd Ingraham) and his accomplice (Boyd), out to steal his gold mine. Following Cooper's victory over Boyd in the bar, the women appear again, Compson pacified and Johnson in Cooper's arms in time for the "happily ever after" fadeout.

It was a role typical of Cooper in his earlier years—the virile, punching hero as comfortable in the saddle as in a woman's arms. He made five other films that year and was well established as a star. *The Spoilers* was big box office and one of the best of the five versions made to date of this Klondike yarn.

Gary Cooper as Glenister

Betty Compson (as Cherry Malotte) and Gary Cooper

Director Edwin Carewe with Kay Johnson and Gary Cooper

16

William ''Stage'' Boyd and Gary Cooper
during their fight

Boyd and the victorious Cooper after their struggle, one of the first realistically violent screen brawls

Min and Bill *(1930, M-G-M) with Marie Dressler*

Wallace Beery (1886–1949)

His moon face, atop a hulking body, was mobile as putty and ugly as mud. His voice, emanating from a mouth that seemed to stretch from ear to ear, sounded a bit like an intoxicated bullfrog. When he was bad he could evoke fear and loathing in an audience; when he was good he assumed a pixieish quality as a lovable rogue who brought laughter and tears from the millions of filmgoers who made him the most popular character actor of the decade.

Like his brother, Noah, he was cast early in his career as a villain. The roles of the sinister Magua in *Last of the Mohicans,* 1920, and of a Hun intent on raping Blanche Sweet in *The Unpardonable Sin,* 1919, were typical. Throughout the early 20s he continued to play mostly toughs. The later 20s saw him in several comedies, but he returned to the bad-guy role as a murderous convict in *The Big House*, 1930, his first talkie. His performance, complete with shambling gait and eerie voice, made the film a sensational success.

His thug image mellowed with subsequent talkies, and he reached his peak as a no-good with a heart of gold. He and the marvelous Marie Dressler delighted audiences in the brawling, guzzling, smooching *Min and Bill*, also 1930, and three years later repeated their fine performances in *Tugboat Annie*. Even more impressive was his performance in *The Champ*, 1931, as an over-the-hill fighter who pulls himself together for a comeback, thanks to the faith and support of his son, little Jackie Cooper. He wins the fight but takes such a beating that he collapses dead in young Cooper's arms in a scene that remains a high spot in film history. The picture brought Beery an Oscar. He shared the best-actor Oscar that year with Fredric March.

Whatever role Beery was given, he supplied huge entertainment. He was a wrestler in *Flesh*, 1932; a wormy businessman in *Grand Hotel*, 1932; a tycoon with political aspirations in *Dinner at Eight*, 1933; the legendary Pancho Villa in *Viva Villa!*, 1934; Long John Silver (again with an adoring Jackie Cooper) in *Treasure Island,* 1934; a thieving trader in *China Seas*, 1935. With good reason he was one of M-G-M's big money-makers throughout the decade.

Wallace Beery (1936)

Viva Villa! (1934, M-G-M), Beery facing firing squad

The Champ *(1931, M-G-M) with Jackie Cooper*

18

Marie Dressler (1869–1934)

Every actor knows that children and animals are notorious scene-stealers. Marie Dressler could outsteal *both* without even half trying. All she had to do was hoist her great hulking frame within camera range, her eyes bulging, glaring, her mouth drawn like a gargoyle's to the very bottom of her substantial jowls, and no other actor, child or beast stood a chance of registering with an audience. No matter how minor her part, she was certain to dominate as long as she was on screen and frequently, as with Norma Shearer in *Let Us Be Gay*, 1930, even when she was off. Whether playing comedy or drama, Dressler was a thunderous performer.

There was never a trace of phoniness about Dressler—off screen as well as on. Whether she was before camera, in rehearsal, playing a benefit or trawling for muskellunge on her beloved St. Lawrence River, where she made her summer home, she was always natural.

Dressler's career lasted 51 years, spanning the legitimate stage, vaudeville, Mack Sennett silent comedies and talking pictures. She co-starred with Chaplin in *Tillie's Punctured Romance*, 1914, and was mildly popular throughout the 20s. However, it was not until sound was introduced that she hit her stride. In 1930 she was brilliantly paired with Wallace Beery in *Min and Bill* and won the best-actress Oscar. These two were such adorable old reprobates, each trying to outslug, outguzzle, outgrimace the other, that audiences clamored for more. In 1933 they were reteamed in *Tugboat Annie*. It was their last work together. That same year Dressler completed *Dinner at Eight* and *Christopher Bean* and insisted she was ''just beginning'' to discover what acting was all about. By 1934, at the peak of her popularity and artistry, she was dead of cancer. After 40 years her brilliance has neither been diminished nor forgotten.

Tugboat Annie *(1933, M-G-M) with* Wallace Beery

Marie Dressler (1930)

Anna Christie *(1930, M-G-M) with George F. Marion*

Emma *(1932, M-G-M)*

Edward G. Robinson as Caesar Enrico Bandello

Little Caesar (1930)

In 1930 advertisements proclaimed ''Little Caesar—King of the Underworld! He ruled supreme—a law unto himself, for in his racket he was court, judge and jury. His verdict was final, for he was also the executioner! He runs the gamut of power—from gutter to gang ruler to gutter again!'' Despite such publicity, critics wrote the film off as just another gangster movie of the genre that had become popular in the late 20s. Yet audiences loved it and its main character, the snarling crime czar Rico (Edward G. Robinson). They delighted in the depiction of the underworld characters and in the almost innocent, nongraphic violence of gangs shooting it out. Audiences recognized that life outside the law was doomed to be short-lived but enjoyed their glimpse of the underworld. Gangster films were exciting escapist fare and offered a change of pace from the sugar-coated musicals that were all but dominating early sound films.

Produced on a shoestring budget, with only workmanlike directorial shaping by Mervyn LeRoy, *Little Caesar* was successful largely because of Edward G. Robinson's unforgettable, razor-edged portrayal of the slimy, terrifying, power-crazed Rico. His characterization was rich in detail, charged with energy. Audiences were unaccustomed to seeing such naturalistic acting. Instead of the excessive, melodramatic histrionics of the actors of the silents and early talkies, Robinson ''lived'' on screen. His voice, his speech patterns suggested nothing of the beware-of-the-microphone self-consciousness that prevailed in most of the early sound films. His final, dying words, ''Mother of Mercy, is this the end of Rico?'' rang with such realism that they are among the most famous in screen history.

Robinson made *Little Caesar* an enduring film classic, and *Little Caesar* made Robinson a star.

Little Caesar at the peak of his power

Edward G. Robinson, Doublas Fairbanks, Jr., and Glenda Farrell

20

The Public Enemy (1931)

"No, gangster pictures are *not* dead—not so long as they produce thrillers like this!" wrote *Photoplay* magazine's film critic in June 1931. This review was not praising *The Public Enemy* but *The Secret Six*, M-G-M's forgotten sequel to *The Big House*. On the magazine's next page the same reviewer said of *The Public Enemy*, " . . . it's just another not-so-hot contribution to gang lore on the screen. Hasn't there been enough?"

Apparently audiences thought not. Like *Little Caesar*, which had been released four months earlier, *The Public Enemy* was a star-maker and pushed James Cagney to the forefront of Hollywood's top names. Audiences adored his cocky, swaggering Tom Powers who ground a grapefruit in Mae Clark's face, shot the horse that had killed his friend and pushed around his molls, Jean Harlow and Joan Blondell.

Cagney's Tom was certainly reprehensible, but he was also oddly appealing. So appealing, in fact, that audiences often found themselves rooting for the "bad guy." This charismatic appeal made the picture's end, when Cagney's dead body, encased in plaster, topples through his mother's doorway, all the more shattering.

Thanks to *Little Caesar* and *The Public Enemy* gangster pictures were far from dead. They had just been infused with new life.

Jean Harlow and James Cagney

James Cagney and Edward Woods

Norma Shearer (1904–)

Canadian-born Norma Shearer reigned throughout the 30s as Hollywood's "first lady." She epitomized elegance and sophistication. Married in 1927 to the brilliant young M-G-M producer Irving Thalberg, the chic brunette naturally had an edge on actresses like Garbo and Crawford when the meatier roles were assigned. But she probably would have gotten most of them even without her husband. A star in silent films, she returned to the screen after a year-and-a-half leave with her first talkie, *The Trial of Mary Dugan*, 1929, proving that she had a bright future in the new sound medium.

With intelligent management from M-G-M's publicity department, Shearer topped most popularity polls during the early 30s. Magazines featured many admiring articles on her private and professional life, revealing her as a model wife and mother, a fashion trend-setter in stylish Adrian clothes and new hair styles and as a patrician beauty with a profile as famous as John Barrymore's. She was always poised, sensitive, dignified.

Shearer conveyed respectability and charm even when playing downbeat roles like that of Jerry in *The Divorcee*, 1930, for which she won an Oscar. Her versatility was demonstrated in films like *The Last of Mrs. Cheney,* 1929, and *A Free Soul*, 1931, whose characters slipped a bit morally—but Shearer could slip on the screen and still be a lady!—and in such classical roles as Juliet in *Romeo and Juliet*, 1936, and Elizabeth Barrett in *The Barretts of Wimpole Street*, 1934. She adroitly did battle with Robert Montgomery as the Noel Coward heroine in *Private Lives*, 1931, and graciously bore Clark Gable's illegitimate child in the film version of Eugene O'Neill's *Strange Interlude*, 1932.

After Thalberg's death in 1936 Shearer still had her choice of roles and her career was at its zenith, but after only five more movies she retired in 1942.

A Free Soul *(1931, M-G-M) with Leslie Howard*

Idiot's Delight *(1939, M-G-M) with Clark Gable*

Smilin' Through *(1932, M-G-M) with Leslie Howard*

The Barretts of Wimpole Street *(1934, M-G-M) with Fredric March*

The Divorcee *(1930, M-G-M) with Robert Montgomery*

City Lights (1931)

This Chaplin classic, like his only other film made during the 30s—*Modern Times*, 1936—was one of the last silent movies. It was a one-man virtuoso performance, with Chaplin as writer, producer, director and star (Virginia Cherrill admirably played the female lead). Its concession to the new era of talkies was the use of realistic sound effects in comic sequences and a haunting, delicate synchronized score that Chaplin also composed.

Once again Chaplin plays his famous creation, the Tramp. The hard-luck, noble Little Fellow encounters and falls in love with a blind flower girl. She mistakes him for a millionaire and offers him a flower, which he solicitously accepts with his last penny. The forlorn romantic by chance rescues a drunken millionaire from drowning. The wealthy gent becomes a generous friend when drunk but doesn't recognize the tramp when sober. Chaplin takes the blind girl under his wing and takes flight with the rich man's money to help restore her sight.

He is sent to prison. Upon his release he looks for the girl and finds her in a flower shop, her sight regained. Seeing his pathetic figure, she comes outside and places a coin in his hand. She recognizes the hands that had placed money in her own and sees he must have suffered terribly to help her. She murmurs, "You?" "You can see now?" he asks imploringly. And pressing his hand in hers, she replies, in what even with subtitles must be one of the most tender, lyrical and stirring scenes in film, "Yes, I can see now."

City Lights wove pathos and comedy with great simplicity of style and story. But each scene was the result of laborious detail and planning. In an early scene Chaplin mocks the talkies and comments on the Depression era as the solemn unveiling of a Statue of Prosperity (with the discourse of the pompous speakers unintelligible) reveals the jobless hero asleep in the arms of the figure. Beneath the bittersweet sentimentalism of Chaplin's films there were many serious overtones, particularly in this crisis decade. *Modern Times* and *The Great Dictator*, 1940, represent the full development of this social concern.

The initial reaction to *City Lights* in the U. S. was not a warm one, and only after Chaplin presented it in Europe did it become popular and commercially successful.

Harry Myers, Charles Chaplin and policeman

The winsome tramp, Charles Chaplin

Charles Chaplin and his eccentric millionaire friend, Harry Myers

24

Charles Chaplin and Virginia Cherrill

Paul Muni (1895–1967)

The Life of Emile Zola *(1937, Warner Brothers)*
with *Gloria Holden*

During the 30s Paul Muni created some of the screen's most penetrating and unforgettable characters. Born in Austria, Muni spent his early years in the United States (from 1908 to 1925) training in the Yiddish theater. In 1929 he moved to films (*The Valiant*) from Broadway, where he was enjoying an enthusiastic critical reception. Three years after his arrival in Hollywood his portrayal of Al Capone in the film *Scarface* brought him stardom. The same year he starred in *I Am a Fugitive from a Chain Gang*, a picture that cemented his fame and won him his first Oscar nomination.

Muni was essentially a character actor, specializing in roles that focused on the man, rarely on Muni the personality. The Muni face was so often hidden behind whiskers, slanted eyes, scars, glasses and makeup that one wondered what he really looked like. Consequently, he was never a star in the Gable–Cooper tradition. One went to see Louis Pasteur or Emile Zola, not Paul Muni. This worked to his disadvantage in the glamour world of Hollywood, but nevertheless he was recognized as an actor of consummate skill and integrity.

From 1932 to 1937 Muni received four best-actor Academy Award nominations. He won the Oscar for his warm, intelligent characterization in *The Story of Louis Pasteur*, 1935. In 1937 Muni scored triumphs with *The Good Earth* and *The Life of Emile Zola*. His sensitive rendering of Zola's agonizing internal conflict regarding the defense of Dreyfus is a testament to Muni's artistic skill. The film won an Oscar, and Muni won the New York Film Critics' best-actor award.

Despite his artistic and box-office successes, two unpopular films in 1939 diminished his popularity, and six years and five so-so films later Muni's film career was virtually ended.

The Life of Emile Zola *(1937, Warner Brothers)*

I Am a Fugitive from a Chain Gang *(1932, Warner Brothers)*

The Story of Louis Pasteur *(1935, Warner Brothers)*

Scarface: Shame of a Nation *(1932, United Artists)*

The Life of Emile Zola *(1937, Warner Brothers)*

Juarez *(1939, Warner Brothers)*

Frankenstein *(1931, Universal) with Boris Karloff*

Horrors!

In 1931 a British-born, intellectually inclined actor, Boris Karloff, appeared in 13 talking pictures. One of them, about a young scientist named Frankenstein (Colin Clive) who fabricates a do-it-yourself mechanical man, featured Karloff as the crew-cut, knobby-faced monster depicted in a novel written more than a century earlier by one of the first feminists, Mary Wollstonecraft Shelley. From that point on, although the majority of his characters were not monsters or ghouls, Karloff was inextricably linked in the public's mind with the scariest of horror films. In addition, people persisted in calling him Frankenstein, forgetting that it was his creator, not the monster, who bore that name.

While Karloff, with his creeping mechanical gait and deathlike visage, was the leading monster of the 30s, a Hungarian-born actor named Bela Lugosi was cornering the ghoul market. Bram Stoker's weird tale of a certain Count Dracula, a vampire with an unquenchable thirst for human blood, had been made into a silent film, *Nosferatu*, in 1922. Years later Lugosi played the sanguinary Count on Broadway, and in 1931 Tod Browning directed the film version. Like Karloff, Lugosi was forever consigned in the public mind to roles of zombies, vampires, monsters and spooks. Black-caped, silky-voiced, sinister-sexy Count Dracula made his daytime home in a coffin. When he slowly emerged from it audiences knew at once that he was ready for action. Directors never showed him actually at work as a vampire. Once the victim's head fell back to expose an alabaster neck, one knew all too well what was going to happen.

There were, of course, many other monsters in the 30s and ghouls and living mummies aplenty, but none as blood-chillingly thrilling as those portrayed by Karloff and Lugosi.

Frankenstein *(1931, Universal) with Boris Karloff*

The Walking Dead *(1936, Warner Brothers) with Boris Karloff and would-be killers*

Dracula *(1931, Universal) with Bela Lugosi*

Mad Love *(1935, M-G-M) with Peter Lorre and Frances Drake*

The Return of Chandu *(1934, Principal Serial) with Bela Lugosi and Dean Benton*

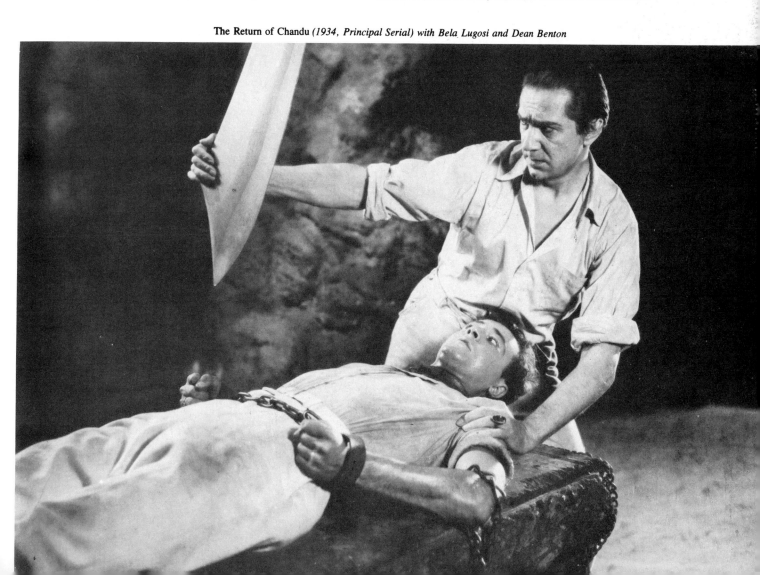

King Kong (1933) and Sci-Fi

It seems there was this uncharted Skull Island in the waters west of Sumatra that was populated by enormous reptiles from the Mesozoic era and one gigantic mammal named King Kong. Kong lived an amiable existence, save for the times he encountered a warlike Brontosaurus or Pterodactyl. The King, who appeared to be no less than 50 feet tall, was in reality an 18-inch foam-rubber-and-steel model who was given life by the superb use of stop-action animation.

His story is simple and touching. Discovered by an expedition that included Bruce Cabot, Robert Armstrong and Fay Wray, Kong is hauled off his island and transported to New York. En route he develops a consuming affection for Wray. Kong tries to make his escape from the city, wrecking it in an attempt, and ends clinging to the Empire State Building with Fay Wray clutched fondly in one hand.

The last scene, in which Kong is finally gunned down from the air (he thoughtfully deposited Fay safely on the tower before the onslaught), was a triumph for the special-effects department.

In the same decade that King Kong took New York by storm, science-fiction appeared on the silver screen. The best of the 30s sci-fi films was the British-made *Things to Come*, 1936. On the American side of the ocean there were only some low-budget Flash Gordon and Buck Rogers films (with Buster Crabbe playing both title roles) which involved baroque-looking spaceships, kingdoms floating on clouds and other sugar-coated views of the future. American studios didn't attempt to cover the market of the future. Perhaps they felt that a view of what was to come was not the stuff to lighten the burdens of a depression-ridden society.

Flash Gordon (1936, Universal serial) with Buster Crabbe

Buck Rogers (1939, Universal serial) with Buster Crabbe

King Kong *(1933, RKO)*

King Kong *(1933, RKO) with Fay Wray*

Irene Dunne and Richard Dix

Cimarron (1931)

Wesley Ruggles directed this sprawling screen treatment of Edna Ferber's chronicle of the Oklahoma Territory from lawless infancy in 1890 to statehood in 1907. *Cimarron* was RKO-Radio Pictures' first major blockbuster at the box office and put it in the major leagues of the Hollywood studio system, just behind M-G-M and Warner Brothers. It also established the standard for epic Western film-making, including the necessary shooting, lynching, robbery and spectacular action scene, in this case the great land rush, with thousands of homesteaders in wagons and on horseback stampeding to stake claims on the free-for-the taking territory. *Cimarron* was awarded an Oscar for best picture, as well as being honored for best writing and best art direction. It also provided Irene Dunne with her first major film role.

The title, derived from the Spanish word for *wild*, is also the name of an Oklahoma river and is an appropriate description of the entire territory, physically and socially. It might also be applied to the hero, Yancey Cravat (Richard Dix), who comes to the territory with his young bride, Sabra (Dunne), and proceeds to bring law and order with his blazing six-shooters and his flaming newspaper editorials. Cravat constantly leaves his family to take up his cudgel against lawlessness and injustice, while the rest of the Cravats wait with exemplary patience for his return. The film ends with Dunne (who made use of her free time and became a Congresswoman) holding Dix in her arms as he dies following his umpteenth heroic deed—the prevention of an oilfield disaster.

Richard Dix and Irene Dunne

Richard Dix, Douglas Scott and Irene Dunne

Richard Dix as Yancey Cravat

Homesteaders race to stake claims during The Great Land Rush

Josef von Sternberg (1894–1969) and Marlene Dietrich (1901–)

They were creator and creation. Von Sternberg's primary concern was "art," which for him meant style, and for this reason Dietrich, a chunky German film and stage actress whom he discovered and cast as Lola, the seductive temptress in *The Blue Angel,* 1930, was his ideal leading lady.

In an age of stars, not directors, Dietrich gradually overshadowed her mentor. After completing the film in Germany, he began to transform her ample, curving silhouette into a shimmering, streamlined mannequin who would arrive in Hollywood and declare herself Garbo's number-one threat in the glamour derby. By 1933 they had produced four other films (*Morocco,* 1930, *Dishonored,* 1931, *Shanghai Express* and *Blonde Venus,* 1932), all over budget, over schedule and only moderate financial successes.

Their films didn't register with the public, so Paramount assigned her to *Song of Songs,* 1933, with Rouben Mamoulian directing.

Dietrich and Von Sternberg made two more films, both box-office disasters. In the latter, *The Devil Is a Woman,* 1935, his flair for elaborately decorating his star had the effect of losing her in the costuming. In 1937 Paramount bought out her contract and she was without work until Universal cast her as a dance-hall gal in a spoofy Western, *Destry Rides Again,* 1939. Von Sternberg's only significant work after their collaboration was *Crime and Punishment,* 1936. As for Dietrich, despite some undistinguished films and a tepid public following (she was more popular among the *literati* and theater folk), she became, with her ambiguous sex image, ageless features and indefatigable verve, a screen immortal.

Shanghai Express *(1932, Paramount)*

The Devil Is a Woman *(1935, Paramount)*

Dishonored *(1931, Paramount) with Victor McLaglen*

34

Blonde Venus *(1932, Paramount) with Cary Grant*

Scarlet Empress *(1934, Paramount) with John Lodge and C. Aubrey Smith*

Bird of Paradise (1932)

When in 1931 *Tabu*, director F. W. Murnau's realistic tale of the South Seas, was released, it proved to be a box-office dud. The next year an artistically inferior picture, *Bird of Paradise*, grossed enormous sums. The reason for the latter's success? It gave the public what it wanted, and that was *not* realism. The film's cast was headed by two Hollywood stars, Dolores Del Rio and Joel McCrea, who cavorted about in seductive costumes that were little more than loincloths and feathers. To this already winning duo director King Vidor added what was fast becoming a 30s cinematic necessity, a form of nature on the rampage. In this case it was a volcano that erupted magnificently.

Made on location in Hawaii, the film is characterized by sweeping views of white beaches, tall mountains, still lagoons, native feasts and mysterious tribal rituals. In this setting the simple love story is revealed with every rise and fall of action and emotion punctuated by Max Steiner's musical score. Del Rio, a native girl, falls in love with McCrea, a foreign adventurer. Her love for the white man is strong and true, but it is also offensive to her gods. Despite McCrea's amorous urgings to the contrary, Del Rio is convinced that the gods are angry with her, and at the film's conclusion she hurls herself into the volcano's fiery maw in expiation for her sin. In 1932 this was a satisfying ending to a film considered grand Hollywood entertainment. But within three years Hollywood had become so sophisticated that no one except producer David O. Selznick seemed willing to admit his connection with it.

Dolores Del Rio in befeathered native costume

Dolores Del Rio as Luana

Joel McCrea (as Johnny Baker) and Dolores Del Rio

Constance Bennett (1905–1965)

''My career as a movie star was virtually handed to me on a silver platter,'' Miss Bennett once told an interviewer. Nevertheless, no one could ever accuse her of having taken it lightly. She was a shrewd business woman and a fine actress who was equally adept at comedy and drama. She also happened to be the eldest of three daughters of Richard Bennett, famous stage actor and early silent-film director and actor. Educated at Miss Shandor's Park Avenue School in New York, Mrs. Merrill's fashionable school in Mamaroneck, New York, and Mme. Balsan's finishing school in Versailles, Miss Bennett appeared in Hollywood looking so cool, blond, lovely and poised that her initial stardom in silent pictures was hardly surprising.

Bed of Roses (1933, RKO) with Joel McCrea

But in 1926 the fiercely independent Bennett abandoned her career to tour Europe with her first husband, whom she rather quickly divorced. When she returned in 1929, talkies were the rage, and she proved herself completely capable of picking up her career and climbing to even greater heights within the early years of the 30s in comedies like *Sin Takes a Holiday,* 1931, and melodramas like *Three Faces East,* 1930, *The Common Law,* 1931, and *Bought,* 1931.

In 1932, although under regular contract to RKO-Radio Pictures, the popular Bennett engineered her way into a one-picture deal with Warner Brothers which netted her the staggering sum of $150,000 for only one month's work.

In 1933–34 she was forced by her studio contract to appear in several unimpressive tearjerkers, and these left her with little bargaining power at all. The next year, considered washed up, she went to England and starred in still another disaster, *Everything Is Thunder,* 1936. In 1937 her career took a sudden upswing when she appeared in *Topper*. After the sequel, *Topper Takes a Trip,* 1938, she appeared in a film the title of which all too painfully described its effect on her career, *Tail Spin,* 1939. Unhappily, the best of Miss Bennett's work was behind her. She had glittered brightly but all too briefly.

Affairs of Cellini (1934, United Artists) with Fredric March

Topper (1937, M-G-M) with Roland Young and Cary Grant

After Office Hours (1935, M-G-M) with Clark Gable

Joan Crawford as Flaemmchen

Grand Hotel (1932)

This granddaddy of the "All-Star" pictures boasted a cast of M-G-M luminaries (Greta Garbo, Wallace Beery, John and Lionel Barrymore, Joan Crawford, Jean Hersholt and Lewis Stone). Based on Vicki Baum's play of life and love on the European plan, the film thrilled audiences despite the ironic truth of Stone's on-screen observation that the Grand Hotel was a place where there are "people coming, people going—always coming and going and nothing ever happens." Because of the stylish manner in which nothing happened, *Grand Hotel* earned best-picture accolades for 1932.

A series of interwoven vignettes supplied enough intrigues and characters to justify at least three movies of equal length. Miss Crawford admirably played an ambitious call girl–secretary tempted to attach herself to an insufferably crude industrialist (Beery). She resists temptation with the help of Lionel Barrymore, a dying bookkeeper who, resolving to go out in style, wins Miss Crawford's affection. Garbo was an aging ballerina saved from suicide by a rejuvenating romance with John Barrymore, who calls himself the Baron but is in fact an appealing scoundrel residing at the hotel only to rob its wealthy guests. She leaves the hotel to meet him at the train station with her flattering illusion intact; but her gaiety is that much more poignant to the audience, who knows that her lover has been killed trying to steal from Beery.

Miss Crawford was the most interesting performer in the film and might have totally dominated it were the real star not the hotel itself. One could not help but be more seduced by its Art Deco interior—the sweeping staircase, balconies, hugely exaggerated lobby, smoked-glass elevator doors and glittering, constantly revolving front door—than by any one of the inhabitants.

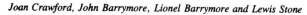

Joan Crawford, John Barrymore, Lionel Barrymore and Lewis Stone

Wallace Beery and Joan Crawford

38

Greta Garbo as Grusinskaya

Greta Garbo with John Barrymore (as Baron Felix von Geigern)

Ten Cents a Dance *(1931, Columbia)*

Barbara Stanwyck (1907–   )

Fate often wiggles its fickle finger in peculiar ways. Why, for example, make Barbara Stanwyck a movie star? With her rather horsey face and mannish figure, she didn't seem the sort of beauty one would ogle on the street. Her acting was usually wooden and mannered. She could cry easily and imitate hysteria with great enthusiasm but seldom with any real fire. Vocally, she rendered English ladies, evangelists, cow queens, missionaries and Irish rebels as though each hailed from Brooklyn (which she did).

But she was always a good—though not a great—box-office attraction and one of the most respected and reliable Hollywood stars. Perhaps the reason was that she worked hard to do her job competently. She was relatively free from pretension, a tomboy next door, everybody's trusted-friend type. Then, too, she was a ferocious fighter. When she failed at sales-clerking at 13, she beat her way up through the ranks of Broadway chorus lines to stardom in her second major role, *Burlesque,* in 1927.

She married Frank Fay, who pushed her career with Warner Brothers and Columbia (which gave her a role in *Mexicali Rose,* 1930), but stardom came when Frank Capra was persuaded she would be good for Columbia's *Ladies of Leisure,* also made in 1930. Naturally, he wanted first to test her, but she adamantly refused, claiming she'd been tested to death. He sent for the two films she had done, liked them and gave her the part.

Stanwyck's unyielding professionalism earned her the respect of colleagues. In the 34 films she made during the 30s, she rarely appeared without a strong male co-star (among them were Robert Taylor, her second husband, Wallace Beery and Herbert Marshall). *Stella Dallas,* 1937, was perhaps her most memorable film. She was downright delightful as the frustrated mother in her frumpy, flowered-print dresses, ankle-strap heels and frizzy hair.

Ever in My Heart *(1933, Warner Brothers) with Otto Kruger*

So Big *(1932, Warner Brothers) with Guy Kibbee and May Madison*

Stella Dallas *(1937, United Artists) with Anne Shirley*

40

The Bitter Tea of General Yen *(1933, Columbia)*

Annie Oakley *(1935, RKO) with Preston Foster*

His Brother's Wife *(1936, M-G-M) with Robert Taylor*

Nana *(1934, United Artists; Samuel Goldwyn) with Phillips Holmes and Anna Sten*

Dorothy Arzner (1902–)

Only one woman directed films in Hollywood during the 30s—Dorothy Arzner. Starting at Paramount Studios as a film cutter and editor of silent pictures, she had her first behind-the-camera experience doing several of the bullfight shots for Valentino's *Blood and Sand* in 1922. With no other directing experience, she was elevated to writer-director of Paramount's *Fashions for Women*, 1927, and produced a hit. She followed it with four other successes, each with a top star like Clara Bow, Nancy Carroll, Richard Arlen and her personal discovery, Fredric March. She so admired March's acting that she starred him in four films: *The Wild Party*, 1929, *Sarah and Son*, 1930, *Honor Among Lovers*, 1931, and *Merrily We Go to Hell*, 1932.

In 1933 Miss Arzner broke Hollywood tradition by declaring herself free of studio affiliation, becoming one of the first independent directors. As such, her first job was at RKO-Radio Pictures, where she saw the young Katharine Hepburn in jungle costume, perched in a tree on the set of what was to be her next film. Miss Arzner pulled her down from her perch, off the set and cast her in *Christopher Strong*, 1933. It was one of the year's finest films and a milestone in the careers of both women.

Samuel Goldwyn hired her to direct *Nana*, 1934, a vehicle designed to introduce Anna Sten as a Garbo rival. The film was interesting, but Miss Sten failed to click with American audiences. Next, Arzner directed *Craig's Wife*, 1936, for Columbia Pictures. Miss Arzner's last film of the decade was M-G-M's disappointing *The Bride Wore Red*, 1937. In the early 40s she directed only two features and retired in 1943.

Merrily We Go to Hell *(1932, Paramount) with cameraman David Abel, Miss Arzner and Sylvia Sidney*

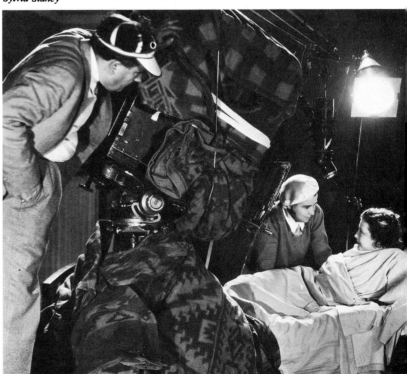

Christopher Strong *(1933, RKO) with Katharine Hepburn and Colin Clive*

George Cukor (1899–   )

After co-directing two films in 1930 with Cyril Gardner and one with Louis Gasnier, George Cukor directed his first feature, *Tarnished Lady*, in 1931, starring Tallulah Bankhead. It marked the start of a long and distinguished career as one of Hollywood's foremost directors. Trained in the theater (he fired Bette Davis from her first stock-company job), he brought his considerable talents to film-making. His emphasis was on his actors and actresses, not on external action. Most of his works were highly literate, narrative pieces with strong central acting roles, usually for women. During the 30s he guided Katharine Hepburn through her screen debut in *A Bill of Divorcement*, 1932, *Little Women*, 1933, *Sylvia Scarlett*, 1935, and *Holiday*, 1938. Both Norma Shearer in *Romeo and Juliet*, 1936, and Greta Garbo in *Camille*, 1937, received Oscar nominations under his direction. He made three films with Constance Bennett—*What Price Hollywood*, 1932, *Rockabye*, 1932, and *Our Betters*, 1933; starred Jeanette MacDonald with Maurice Chevalier in *One Hour with You*, 1932 (Ernst Lubitsch co-director); put W. C. Fields in *David Copperfield*, 1935; and cast Claudette Colbert as *Zasa*, 1939. Four Cukor films received Oscar nominations for best picture: *One Hour with You*, *Little Women*, *David Copperfield* and *Romeo and Juliet*. James Stewart was the first performer to win an Oscar under his direction for *The Philadelphia Story*, 1940. Ingrid Bergman was the second in *Gaslight*, 1944. His last film before retirement at the age of 70 was *Justine*, 1969.

Little Women *(1933, RKO) with Cukor and Katharine Hepburn*

Sylvia Scarlett *(1935, RKO) with Brian Aherne, Katharine Hepburn, Cary Grant and Natalie Paley*

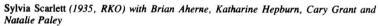

Tarnished Lady *(1931, Paramount) with Clive Brook, Elizabeth Patterson and Tallulah Bankhead*

Publicity shot of Mae West (1933)

Mae West (1892–) and W. C. Fields (1879–1946)

These top-flight comedy stars of the 30s were masters of self-parody. Impervious to ridicule and critical put-downs (except their own), they possessed such massive egos that together they could fill the Grand Canyon, with enough surplus to flood the entire Pacific Northwest. Her hourglass figure and platinum-blond hair and his bulbous nose, squinty eyes and rotund middle were easily caricatured. Their idiosyncratic voices—hers arrogantly gutsy, his creaking and nasal—were often imitated, but their humor was distinctly original, impertinent and decidedly raunchy.

Mae West was a splendidly vulgar sex symbol who rode roughshod over lovers and entranced audiences with legendary quips like "When I'm good, I'm very, very good. But when I'm bad, I'm better." She wrote the scripts for most of the eight films she starred in during the 30s and is best remembered for *Klondike Annie* and *Go West Young Man,* 1936, and *My Little Chickadee,* 1939. Except for *Myra Breckinridge* in 1970, she last appeared in *The Heat's On* in 1943.

Fields specialized in loathing children and dogs as well as hurling insults at anyone so unfortunate as to be near him. With indiscriminate, though endearing, guile he played salesmen, bank managers, motorists, policemen and impresarios. His nose was but one of the many subjects that inspired him to solemn observation. "Some are born with big noses. Others acquire them. Mine is cultivated!" he boasted. And no doubt the whiskey he drank nonstop on the sets aided in that process.

An expert juggler and a *Ziegfeld Follies* star before entering the movies in 1915, he fully bloomed only in the 30s in such comic delights as *The Old-Fashioned Way* and *It's a Gift,* 1934, and in the early 40s with *The Bank Dick* and *My Little Chickadee,* 1940, and *Never Give a Sucker an Even Break,* 1941, all of which he wrote himself. He avidly chose bizarre names for his scripts and insisted they were all taken from life. He found Mr. Prettiwillie on a billboard, Posthlewhistle was an English village, Chester Snaveley an undertaker he knew in Washington and Sned Smunn a lawyer. His favorites were characters from Dickens novels, and in playing one of these, Mr. Micawber in *David Copperfield,* 1935, he gave his most sober, least ribald performance.

Candid shot of W. C. Fields (1935)

David Copperfield (1935, M-G-M) with Freddie Bartholomew

Noah Beery, Sr., and Mae West in She Done Him Wrong *(1933, Paramount)*

Edward G. Robinson (1893–1973) and James Cagney (1904–   )

Edward G. Robinson and James Cagney in Smart Money *(1931, Warner Brothers)*

There is good reason to link Cagney and Robinson together. On screen they most often portrayed toughs and gangsters, while off screen they were the total antitheses to their screen images. Both were intellectual and led quiet lives, which stymied gossip columnists seeking juicy items.

In 1929, Robinson made his first talkie, *Hole in the Wall*, playing a gangster. He was a hoodlum in four of the six pictures he made in 1930. The last of these, *Little Caesar* (see page 20), made him a star. Throughout the 30s Robinson was usually cast as a gangster, a retired gangster or an almost gangster. Occasionally he was offered a change of pace, as in *A Lady to Love*, 1932, and *I Loved a Woman*, 1933. Twice he was even on the right side of the badge, in *Bullets and Ballots*, 1936, and *I Am the Law*, 1938. One of his best pictures in the 30s was *The Whole Town's Talking*, 1935, in which he played both the good and the bad in a dual role. Robinson proved himself equally adept at drama, melodrama and comedy, an accomplishment he shared with his friend Cagney.

James Cagney began his show-biz career as a song-and-dance man in vaudeville and in several Broadway musicals. His big break, a co-starring role (as a murderer) with Joan Blondell in *Penny Arcade*, brought him and Blondell to Hollywood for the film version of *Sinner's Holiday*, 1930. He made three more films that year, but it wasn't until 1931, when he appeared in *Public Enemy* (see page 21), that he made the big time. Though he played many gangsters, Cagney appeared in other guises as well. He was a high-powered press agent in *Hard to Handle*, 1933, a singing theatrical producer in *Footlight Parade*, 1933, and an airline pilot in *Ceiling Zero*, 1936. Perhaps the most unconventional bit of casting ever was giving Cagney the role of Bottom in *A Midsummer Night's Dream*, 1935 (see page 68). Cagney finished the decade off with one of the last big gangster pictures made, *The Roaring Twenties*, 1939.

Edward G. Robinson and victim in Tiger Shark *(1932, Warner Brothers)*

James Cagney and henchmen in The Roaring Twenties *(1939, Warner Brothers)*

Edward G. Robinson and friend in Smart Money *(1931, Warner Brothers)*

Clive Brook and Diana Wynyard as Robert and Jane Marryot

Cavalcade (1933)

Cavalcade opens and closes with a toast. The first occurs on New Year's Eve 1899. Robert, head of the Marryot household, is preparing to leave England to serve in the Boer War. Some 30 years, another war and several personal tragedies later, the Marryots again offer one another a toast over a background of "Auld Lang Syne." *Cavalcade* records these and the events of the years that intervene—Queen Victoria's death, the *Titanic*'s sinking, World War I. The remarkable feat of the film is that these events are put in the context of the characters' lives and are seen from a personal, rather than a historical, view. The Marryots feel personally bereaved by their Queen's death, one of their sons goes down with the *Titanic* and the other is killed in World War I. Audiences came to see this warm, believable family, to share their joys and sorrows. They were intrigued by them.

The film stars Diana Wynyard (who received an Academy Award nomination for her performance) and Clive Brook as the valiant Marryots. They are ably aided by a supporting (mostly British) cast that includes Ursula Jeans, Herbert Munden, Una O'Connor, Beryl Mercer, Bonita Granville and even Betty Grable (in a bit part designated as "girl on couch"). In addition to the fine cast, the film presented an amazingly accurate and atmospheric London—amazing because the film was entirely shot in California. It was also one of the few serious plays written by the usually urbane and comedic Noel Coward.

Cavalcade was the biggest money-maker of 1933, grossing three and a half million dollars. It won itself the Academy Award and rave notices in the United States and, somewhat surprisingly, since it was after all an import, equally good reception in Britain.

Una O'Connor, Diana Wynyard and Clive Brook

John Warburton as Edward Marryot and Margaret Lindsay as Edith Harris

Little Women (1933)

Little Women, based on Louisa May Alcott's durable classic, not only confirmed that Katharine Hepburn, who played Jo, was a star but also earned $110,000 in *one week* at Radio City Music Hall. Its extraordinary success opened the door for period films in general and established its director, George Cukor, as a man who understood the subtleties of translating a classic work of fiction to the screen. When RKO first asked David Selznick to undertake this production—he left for M-G-M before the film was actually made—there was talk of modernizing it. What RKO had in mind was never made specific. One can only wonder what would have happened if this enduring story, set in the 1860s, had somehow suffered that fate known as updating.

Snowman and Katharine Hepburn

Co-starring with Hepburn were Joan Bennett as Amy, Frances Dee as Meg, Jean Parker as Beth, Spring Byington as Marmee and Edna May Oliver as Aunt March. The cast gave convincing life to a tale that lacked both heroes and villains. They made an absolutely normal family believable. Hepburn's Jo glowed with an independence that struck all the right notes. When she looked out at life and exclaimed, "Look at me, World, I'm Jo March, and I'm so happy!" audiences knew she was telling the truth.

The revelation provided by *Little Women* was that film versions of classics need not be approached with solemnity. George Cukor's direction, described by one critic as "easygoing," revealed confidence in both the material and the actors. His control of character and movement never faltered. The adventures of these nice little ladies and their nice widowed mother enraptured audiences. They and their environment were a relief from the harsh realities of the Depression. The story was confirmation that young America was a decent nation with upright, hard-working people. Audiences went away convinced that being good was not only an admirable virtue; it was also a source of happiness.

Katharine Hepburn as Jo

Frances Dee as Meg, Jean Parker as Beth and Joan Bennett as Amy

Joan Bennett, Katharine Hepburn and Frances Dee

47

Stage Door *(1937, RKO) with Ginger Rogers*

Holiday *(1938, Columbia) with Cary Grant*

Katharine Hepburn (1909–   )

When Katharine Hepburn left Broadway and arrived in Hollywood in 1932 with a contract for $1,500 per week at RKO, her astonishingly unorthodox manner and appearance so shocked studio officials that one executive exclaimed, "We're paying $1,500 for *that*?" She hardly fit the image of a typical 30s starlet, with her skinny, boyish figure, dark red hair, freckles and personality that seemed designed to shock. She was such an oddity that the studio was on the verge of sending her back to New York when director George Cukor saw one of her screen tests and insisted she be cast in the plum role of John Barrymore's daughter in *A Bill of Divorcement,* 1932. Hepburn turned in a fine performance that was lauded by critics and won from Barrymore the assessment that she was the most important new talent on the screen.

In 1933 she starred in *Christopher Strong, Morning Glory,* for which she won the best-actress Oscar, and *Little Women,* for which she was named best actress at the Venice Film Festival. These successes were followed by the disappointing *Spitfire,* 1934, and a return to Broadway in the fiasco *The Lake.* She was in two more unimpressive films before winning her second Oscar nomination for *Alice Adams,* 1935. Her next three films did not do well at the box office, and even the success of *Stage Door,* 1937, and *Bringing Up Baby,* 1938, was not able to rescue her from the Motion Picture Exhibitors' "box-office poison" list.

When her studio offered her a role in a B picture, Hepburn bought out her contract and went to Columbia for *Holiday,* 1938. That film was good but not good enough to redeem her at the box office. The downswing in her career, combined with the rejection of her bid for the role of Scarlett O'Hara in *Gone with the Wind,* caused Hepburn to return to Broadway to play the lead in *The Philadelphia Story.* The play was a great hit and marked a turning point in her career. Her starring role in the film version, 1940, would boost her to the top again and start the next decade for her with another Oscar nomination.

Alice Adams *(1935, RKO) with Fred MacMurray*

Mary of Scotland *(1936, RKO) with Douglas Walton, John Carradine and lady-in-waiting*

Bringing Up Baby *(1938, RKO) with Cary Grant*

Break of Hearts *(1935, RKO) with Charles Boyer*

Jean Harlow as Kitty Packard

Dinner at Eight (1933)

Dinner at Eight, the film version of the George S. Kaufman–Edna Ferber play, retains all the caustic wit, pathos and crackling dialogue of the original. It is the story of a dinner party given for two honored guests who never turn up. Each of the other guests is revealed to the audience as he or she prepares for the gala. By the time the dinner party is assembled at the table of host Oliver Jordan (Lionel Barrymore), the audience knows who they are and why they have chosen to accept Jordan's invitation.

As was proven by an earlier film—*Grand Hotel*, 1932—nothing glitters quite like a screen full of stars. *Dinner at Eight* follows this success formula. There is John Barrymore as a down-at-the-heels actor, Billie Burke as a social-climbing hostess, Marie Dressler as an acerb great lady of the theater, Wallace Beery as a self-made, two-fisted tycoon and Jean Harlow as his cheaply glamorous, wisecracking wife. The stars are supported by a substantial cast that includes Edmund Lowe, Madge Evans, Louise Closser Hale and Elizabeth Patterson. These diverse personalities create a dinner conversation that is replete with scathing remarks, bright humor and poignant revelations.

Dinner at Eight was an unqualified box-office and critical success. *The New York Times* reviewed it as "one of those rare pictures which keeps you in your seat until the final fade-out, for nobody wants to miss one of the scintillating lines." More than 40 years later this assessment still rings true. When the film ends, the viewer feels he's been to one heck of a party.

Marie Dressler as Carlotta Vance and Lionel Barrymore as Oliver Jordan

Jean Harlow and Wallace Beery, Kitty and Dan Packard

Marie Dressler

Grant Mitchell, George Baxter, Louise Closser Hale, Jean Harlow, Wallace Beery, Edmund Lowe, Karen Morley, Billie Burke

Design for Living (1933)

Gary Cooper and Miriam Hopkins

Many purists considered Ben Hecht's screenplay of Noel Coward's stage comedy a complete failure. He retained but one line of Mr. Coward's text, the toast "For the good of our immortal souls!" but under Ernst Lubitsch's direction the adaptation was in many ways an improvement on the original.

With Gary Cooper and Fredric March in the roles played on the stage by Mr. Coward and Alfred Lunt respectively, the film had a decidedly less esthetic, more virile basis for the rivalry between best friends finding themselves in love with the same girl. As the modern young woman sharing their domicile, Miriam Hopkins conveyed a sense of individuality and genuine dedication to her "loves" that was missing in Lynn Fontanne's stylish, sophisticated stage character. Script and direction both captured the risqué, double-entendre tones of the plot and also suggested significant social and philosophical implications in the characters' dilemma. When, fed up with the jealousy and possessiveness of the two men, Hopkins moves out and marries her boss, she is rejecting their chauvinistic attitudes more than either of them personally. Yet the film concludes with Miss Hopkins deciding to return to a life of "platonic love" with Cooper and March. Marriage was boring compared to the painful but exhilarating life among free souls. It may not have been unadulterated Noel Coward, but it was superb Hecht, Lubitsch, Cooper, Hopkins and March.

Fredric March as Otto, Miriam Hopkins as Gilda and Gary Cooper as Leo

Twentieth Century (1934)

This screen adaptation of the Hecht–MacArthur stage hit was one of the first screwball comedies. Forty years later it's still among the best.

Time is running out for Oscar Jaffe, a down-at-the-heels theatrical producer who must convince the incomparable Lilly Garland to star in his next play before the crack streamliner, the Twentieth Century, arrives in Chicago from New York. If she says yes, he'll never again insult her or make her unhappy. Lilly finds this hard to believe, because she once married Oscar, when she was Mildred Plotka, and though he did make her a star, the transformation left its share of bruises. A hilarious duel ensues, and with John Barrymore brandishing one sword and Carole Lombard another, audiences had the time of their lives. Oscar Jaffe is obviously a conniving rascal who cares only about saving his own skin, but Garland does owe him a lot, so why does she explode every time he starts his pitch—screeching, pacing up and down, throwing people out of her drawing room, behaving, in fact, much like her ex-husband?

Carole Lombard and John Barrymore

Director Howard Hawks was fortunate to have in Barrymore a leading man who loved satirizing the theater and in Carole Lombard a sexy, sinewy actress fully on a par with Barrymore's slippery entrepreneur. It was her role in *Twentieth Century* that made her a Hollywood star. Nothing gets to her, particularly men like Jaffe, who go white as chalk, clutch their throats and gasp, ''I made you, you ungrateful wretch! I made you!''

The rest of the cast—the agents, lawyers, sheriffs, religious nuts, detectives and ubiquitous train conductors who slip in and out of the action like toast constantly popping out of some giant toaster gone haywire—provides a way out of the couple's badgering. Invariably Barrymore or Lombard turns on them, and the audience begins to realize that beneath their steel-jacketed hearts those two like each other. In the mid-30s, when audiences were starved for movies that lifted them out of their everyday woes, a comedy spoof on theatrical life was the best present of all.

John Barrymore as Oscar Jaffe

Ralph Forbes as George Smith, Carole Lombard as Lilly Garland and John Barrymore as Oscar Jaffe

John Barrymore checking his rising temperature

Carole Lombard (1908–1942)

Given a choice between seeing Garbo's best film and Lombard's worst, more than a few discriminating filmgoers would unhesitatingly choose Lombard's. She was sexy. She was natural. She had intelligence, warmth, glamour, wit, humor and enormous talent. She was the total artist—dedicated, aspiring, always growing. She had a unique comic style that made you laugh, and a special, almost Chaplinesque, approach to drama that made you cry.

Early training in Mack Sennett two-reelers led to roles in such so-what efforts as *The Arizona Kid,* 1930. That year she also played opposite William Powell in two films, *Man of the World* and *Ladies Man.* They decided to join forces off screen as well and were married in 1931. For the next four years Lombard played a variety of roles, then in 1934 got her first big break in the hugely funny Hecht–MacArthur classic *Twentieth Century* (see page 53).

Miss Lombard had to wait two years more for another great comedy, *My Man Godfrey,* co-starring her ex-husband, William Powell (they were divorced in 1933). The film has been called the funniest comedy of the decade, although there are those who staunchly maintain that the title goes to *Nothing Sacred,* 1937. Both films helped to make her the highest paid star in 1937.

Two years later she and Clark Gable were married. Their ideal marriage ended in 1942 when he asked her to sell war bonds in Indiana. She never returned. Her plane crashed, killing Carole, her mother and 15 young Army pilots. She was just 34 years old.

No Man of Her Own *(1932, Paramount) with Clark Gable*

Made for Each Other *(1939, Selznick International, United Artists) with James Stewart*

Bolero *(1934, Paramount) with George Raft*

Brief Moment *(1933, Columbia) with Gene Raymond*

True Confession *(1937, Paramount) with Fred MacMurray*

My Man Godfrey *(1936, Universal) with William Powell*

George Arliss, Loretta Young and Robert Young

The House of Rothschild (1934)

When Darryl F. Zanuck left Warners to found his own company, Twentieth Century, he took with him veteran actor George Arliss and cast him as two members of the extraordinary Rothschild family in one of the new studio's first productions. His dual performance and a final Technicolor scene of a royal reception were the high points in this straightforward biography.

The Arliss name had been made portraying immortals such as Voltaire, Hamilton and Disraeli in *Disraeli*, for which he won the best-actor award in 1929. His two Rothschilds were father Mayer, the Frankfurt founder of the financial empire, and son Nathan, an Englishman and the principal successor. Along with the actors who played the other family members, Arliss gives a compelling impression of the strong blood ties within this multinational family, and it is perhaps this sense of kinship that makes the story of their prosperity so convincing and sympathetic.

The story might easily have collapsed into a tale of money and accumulated wealth, but Arliss, through his ability to make audiences "see" his characters and their motivation, elevates the action to the level of human drama. He may be one of the wealthiest, most powerful men in the world, but he is also a father and husband aware of personal and professional responsibilities. Rothschild's triumph, as the film tells it, was not being acknowledged the world's richest man but being someone who expressed his patriotism through the only means at his disposal: unflinching financial support of England's struggle against Napoleon. He thus becomes a great statesman, and England's victory is Rothschild's as well.

Robert Young as Captain Fitzroy and Loretta Young as Julie

Boris Karloff as Count Ledrantz and George Arliss as Rothschild

56

The Lost Patrol (1934)

Strong characterizations and the device of an unseen enemy rescue *The Lost Patrol* from overripe melodrama. Filmed by director John Ford in the California desert, the film has a realistic feeling that was described by *The New York Times* as "an impressive conception of the agony of thirst and also of the scorching heat. . . ."

The film, based on Philip MacDonald's novel *Patrol*, is the story of British cavalrymen lost in the desert and relentlessly pursued by seemingly disembodied Arab sharpshooters. The leader of the patrol is felled by a bullet as the film begins, and Victor McLaglen, the sergeant, becomes leader of the ragged band. The film is an interesting character study of the eleven remaining men, among whom is a fiery-eyed, Bible-quoting madman (Boris Karloff), a gruff pessimist (J. M. Kerrigan) and a typical British gentleman (Reginald Denny).

The viewer soon comes to realize that the men are not just pursued by a human enemy, but by destiny. The story becomes more stirring with this knowledge that the men are attempting to cheat death. One by one the men fall victim until McLaglen alone remains. The sergeant defeats death because he is the only one of the troop who retains a sense of duty, form and military preparedness. But his is a Pyrrhic victory; there is no glory for a leader who has watched his entire patrol die one by one.

The Lost Patrol is not always entirely believable, but the fast-paced action, effective photography and enjoyable, if slightly overdone, performances made it a box-office success. It was also one of the films of the 30s that established an international reputation for director John Ford.

Victor McLaglen and Howard Wilson

Boris Karloff, Victor McLaglen and Wallace Lord

Victor McLaglen, the patrol's only survivor

It Happened One Night (1934)

Nobody except the celebrated director-writer team of Frank Capra and Robert Riskin wanted to make this film. It was a miracle that it was produced at all. Yet it is the father of all sexy-situation comedies and still the best. It made a clean sweep of all five major Oscars (best picture, actor, actress, director and screenplay). No other film holds that honor. No matter if national critics were at odds about its merits, audiences everywhere loved it.

The plot was simple, the laughs and appeal endless. An obstinate rich girl (Claudette Colbert) deserts her father's yacht and meets a roving, rascally reporter on a bus bound for New York. In the name of economy they hitchhike together and share the same motel room, hanging a blanket on a clothesline to separate their beds. He leaves her to sell the story of her flight from wealth. She boils over, but after several twists they make amends and marry. In 1934 this amounted to pretty hot doings!

The dialogue and situations were witty and risqué, yet never raw. There was open, titillating charm in scenes that cleverly challenged old taboos: Colbert hiking up her skirts to get them a ride; Gable removing his shirt, revealing a bare chest; or again Colbert slipping out of her underclothes without ever being seen (except as she placed them one at a time on the "wall" between their beds) and putting on a pair of *his* pajamas. Throughout, Capra creates a feeling of authenticity and urgency by fast-paced location shooting on busses, in motels and on highways. The acting is superb. Gable and Colbert were never better.

Capra contended that a funnier film could have been made about the making of this film. It would have been a documentary on the obstacles in movie-making. There were difficulties selling the original idea (two mediocre "bus" pictures had already flopped); problems in casting (Myrna Loy, Margaret Sullavan and Robert Montgomery adamantly refused the lead roles); pressures of time and weather (outdoor shooting had to be hurried before the onset of winter); budgetary worries (Colbert demanded double her usual salary); and coping with "star" temperaments. Nevertheless it was a profitable blockbuster and made fledgling Columbia Pictures a prime force in Hollywood.

Clark Gable and Claudette Colbert

Clark Gable and Claudette Colbert

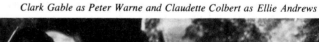
Clark Gable as Peter Warne and Claudette Colbert as Ellie Andrews

Hitchhikers Clark Gable and Claudette Colbert

Bette Davis in her restaurant uniform

Of Human Bondage (1934)

Mildred Rogers, the sluttish waitress, was the first significant role of Bette Davis' career. Other actresses had fared badly with Somerset Maugham characters, but in the role of Mildred the popeyed, blondish ingénue from New England proved she could act. Credit must also go to director John Cromwell for so wisely trusting the then unproven instincts of Miss Davis to make Mildred an unglamorized, realistic character. ''I don't give a damn how I look or what I do on the screen . . . belief is the main thing!'' Davis exclaimed to an interviewer. And believable she was. She brought Mildred to life—pathetic, frightening and wholly human. Miss Davis made audiences understand Mildred's neurotic, complex personality; her mindless thirst for jewelry, furs, good times; her inability to sympathize with the sufferings of others and her blind selfishness.

Miss Davis dominated the film. When she was off screen the focus fell on Leslie Howard, and his story was thoroughly boring. Rather than telling Maugham's tale about a crippled medical student (Howard) who falls hopelessly in love with a tart, the film becomes the portrait of a cheap, frivolous, conniving woman whose calculated flirtations with Howard are only the beginning of her struggle to find money, position, comfort and who, once she has almost attained her goal, is thrust back into the gutter, where she dies of syphilis.

Mr. Howard did little more than mope about, projecting an embarrassing variety of inner anguishes. Yet, in true Hollywood fashion, *his* name was placed above the title.

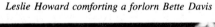

Leslie Howard comforting a forlorn Bette Davis

Leslie Howard and a glamorized, if hardened, Bette Davis

Bette Davis as Mildred Rogers and Leslie Howard as Philip Carey

Leslie Howard and Frances Dee, who plays Sally Athelny

Tarzan

When author Edgar Rice Burroughs killed off Lord and Lady Graystoke and left their infant son and heir to be raised in the jungles of Africa by the ape Ahtu and related lower primates, he launched a major world industry—books, comic strips and movies based on the life and achievements of Tarzan of the Apes.

The first Tarzan, Elmo Lincoln, appeared in the silents. Many years later Buster Crabbe, Herman Brix and Glen Morris, among others, played the part. In between was the one and only "real" Tarzan—Johnny Weissmuller.

Weissmuller's *Tarzan the Ape Man* appeared in 1932 and set the pattern for all who were to follow. His jungle world was beautified by the presence of Maureen O'Sullivan, who deserted a safari to co-star with Johnny in six Tarzan films. In 1939 the treehouse duo became a trio in *Tarzan Finds a Son,* with Johnny Sheffield playing Boy.

All of the Tarzan movies of the 30s, as well as the ones that followed, have a plot or subplot that involved Tarzan and his simian and elephant pals being pitted against assorted evildoers—diamond smugglers or the like—and conquering them and their nefarious schemes. The formula obviously worked. At the end of the 30s and well into the 40s (when he made eight additional jungle films) Weissmuller's Tarzan was still going strong, even after O'Sullivan's 1942 decision to trade in her animal skins permanently for street clothes.

Tarzan the Apeman (1932, M-G-M) with Johnny Weissmuller

Tarzan the Apeman (1932, M-G-M) with Maureen O'Sullivan and Johnny Weissmuller

Tarzan the Apeman *(1932, M-G-M) with Johnny Weissmuller,*
Maureen O'Sullivan and Neil Hamilton

Tarzan the Apeman *(1932, M-G-M) with Maureen O'Sullivan and*
Johnny Weissmuller

Tarzan Escapes *(1936, M-G-M) with Johnny Weissmuller and*
Maureen O'Sullivan

Tarzan Finds a Son *(1939, M-G-M) with Johnny Weissmuller,*
Maureen O'Sullivan and Johnny Sheffield

The Last Days of Pompeii (1935)

*Basil **Rathbone** as Pontius Pilate and Preston Foster as Marcus*

The mere title of this Paramount release promised a disaster of unmatched excitement and terror. Under the direction of Ernest B. Schoedsack, who two years before co-directed *King Kong*, the film realized all of its cataclysmic potential. Audiences not only witnessed the ruin of an entire city but were drawn into the everyday lives of the city's inhabitants.

The film starred Basil Rathbone as Pontius Pilate and Preston Foster as a Pompeian blacksmith who dreams of fame in gladiatorial combat. The lives of these socially unequal residents of Pompeii unravel separately but become intertwined as magisterial Rathbone watches Foster fight for his life in the arena. Yet nature is stronger than caste; before the onslaught of the fiery volcano, men, even Roman administrators, are reduced to a common level of helplessness.

The stuff of disaster movies easily fills the screen with the visual material for gripping melodrama. Against this apocalyptic background they usually focus in on one man's struggle. In *The Last Days of Pompeii* the dramatic excitement achieves a strong balance. Audiences cared about the blacksmith as much as they anguished over the destruction of Pompeii.

Gladiatorial games

Pompeii during the eruption of Vesuvius

The Thin Man *(1934, M-G-M) with Myrna Loy and William Powell*

William Powell (1892–) **and** Myrna Loy (1905–)

William Powell and Myrna Loy were both film veterans with more than 50 films each to their credit when they made *The Thin Man*, 1934, and attained stardom. Throughout the 20s and in the early 30s Powell made a name for himself as a debonair heavy with a variety of characterizations, including con men, villains, seducers and detectives, but it was not until *The Thin Man* that his comedic talent was fully revealed. In that film he combined his charm and special kind of class with true comic flair and won himself a new place in the Hollywood lineup and an Academy Award nomination.

Myrna Loy also began her screen career in the silent 20s, playing Oriental vamps and half-breed sirens who lured men to their destruction. In the early 30s she switched to glamour girls, models and best friends who were usually smart, decorative and fickle. Her uninteresting voice and inexpressive face made her rather weak for straight dramatic roles, but, as she proved most clearly in *The Thin Man*, in comic parts she was delightful.

Powell and Loy had a similar appeal. They were glamorous without being inaccessible, forceful without being overpowering and accomplished without being perfect. The average moviegoer could, and did, identify with them. Largely because of this appeal *The Thin Man* grossed two million in 1934 and marked the first in a series of co-starring roles for Powell and Loy, including five more of the *Thin Man* series as well as such hits as *Evelyn Prentice*, 1934, *Libeled Lady*, 1936, and *The Great Ziegfeld*, 1936. The charm, wit and style of the Powell–Loy team pervaded their pictures, gave them warmth and lightness and made their films ideal escapist fare.

Another Thin Man, 1939, rounded out the 30s for William Powell and Myrna Loy, who each had awaiting in the future 20 additional films.

The Emperor's Candlesticks *(1937, M-G-M) with Luise Rainer*

Rendezvous *(1935, M-G-M) with Rosalind Russell*

Reckless *(1935, M-G-M) with Jean Harlow*

A Connecticut Yankee *(1931, Fox) with Will Rogers*

The Mask of Fu Manchu *(1932, M-G-M) with Charles Starrett*

The Barbarian *(1933, M-G-M) with Ramon Novarro*

Wings in the Dark *(1935, Paramount) with Cary Grant*

A Midsummer Night's Dream

(1935)

A Midsummer Night's Dream was produced by famed European impresario Max Reinhardt. It was his first film, and he was determined to create as lavish a rendition of Shakespeare's comedy as the medium might allow. Reinhardt nominated himself the director, to be assisted by William Dieterle. He chose his stars not so much with regard to the needs of the play—who would best portray Lysander?—but in terms of the Hollywood firmament. He brought lovely Olivia de Havilland from the stage and cast her in her first film role, Hermia. He then cast James Cagney as Bottom, Joe E. Brown as Flute, Hugh Herbert as Snout, Arthur Treacher as Ninny's Tomb, Dick Powell as Lysander, Jean Muir as Helena, Ian Hunter as Theseus and Victor Jory as Oberon, the King of the Fairies. Puck was portrayed by (who else but) Mickey Rooney.

Critical opinion of the film was clearly divided. Some felt that the film industry had no business tampering with anything as lofty as Shakespeare. Others deplored the casting of Cagney, Brown and Powell in Shakespearean roles. On the other hand, there were those who felt Cagney vindicated the daring casting. "So sensitive, so dramatic, and so sure of his rendering . . ." was the way critic John Marks appraised the performance. Another critic, however, wrote, "I would rather die than admit that Mr. Cagney is not a great actor. . . . I must blame it on Shakespeare or Reinhardt." Warner Brothers simply ignored the reviews, mounted a gigantic publicity campaign and by year's end reported that *A Midsummer Night's Dream* had grossed $1,500,000.

Olivia de Havilland as Hermia and Dick Powell as Lysander

Olivia de Havilland, the Queen of the Fairies

Hugh Herbert, Dewey Robinson, Otis Harlan, James Cagney, Arthur Treacher and Frank McHugh

68

Errol Flynn (1909–1959)

"I allow myself to be known as a colorful fragment in a drab world," Flynn once declared. And he certainly was. Never pretending to be an actor, he concentrated on projecting his delightful personality, good looks and athletic agility. From his first starring role in *Captain Blood*, 1935 (with Olivia de Havilland), he epitomized the high-riding, carousing, swashbuckling hero, both on and off screen. His life was so peppered with outrageous and suspect shenanigans (such as slave trading in New Guinea) that Warner Brothers' publicity men worked overtime trying to tone down his public image rather than make it more scintillating.

In 1936 he starred, again with De Havilland, in the successful film *The Charge of the Light Brigade*. The next year he was so firmly established in the image of a suave, sophisticated lady-killer with irresistible physical charms that he was typecast as *The Perfect Specimen*, a silly but amusing comedy. After this he starred as the roguish, storybook hero in *The Adventures of Robin Hood*, 1938, again with his favorite co-star, Olivia de Havilland. They became the day's most popular romantic screen duo (of the unsophisticated variety).

So long as the emphasis was on action and romance, Flynn's pictures were thoroughly enjoyable. However, if he was required to do more than caress swooning damsels and sword-fight, his limitations were glaringly obvious. In *The Private Lives of Elizabeth and Essex*, 1939, he was decidedly lost, playing even the most intense moments as though suppressing laughter. His great good humor seemed all-pervasive.

Flynn's career took a downward turn when, in 1942, two girls under the legal age of eighteen took the wind out of his sails by charging him with statutory rape. The court case, in addition to the loss of De Havilland as a co-star and a dispute with Michael Curtiz, his longtime director, affected his performances. His acting became strained, almost maudlin. One prefers to remember him during his heyday, when he was an audacious, rascally, beautifully free spirit.

The Charge of the Light Brigade (*1936, Warner Brothers) with Olivia de Havilland*

The Prince and the Pauper (*1937, Warner Brothers) with Bobby Mauch*

The Adventures of Robin Hood (*1938, Warner Brothers)*

The Perfect Specimen (*1937, Warner Brothers) with Joan Blondell*

Errol Flynn in his debut role

Captain Blood (1935)

Warner Brothers originally planned *Captain Blood* as a vehicle for Robert Donat, who had scored a hit playing *The Count of Monte Cristo*, 1934. When contract negotiations fizzled a 26-year-old contract player, newly arrived from Tasmania, named Errol Flynn was given the title role, and a new swashbuckling star in the Douglas Fairbanks, Sr., tradition was born. Flynn co-starred with Olivia de Havilland, and together they made such a beautiful, romantic, costumed couple that a new screen love team came into being. They subsequently made seven films together, three in the 30s.

Released only one month after M-G-M's *Mutiny on the Bounty*, this production proved that sea epics need not necessarily be filmed on location with enormous budgets. While the M-G-M crews were off in Tahiti running up production costs, the technicians at Warners were constructing inexpensive miniature ships and filming them in a tank on the back lot. Mock-ups of the ships' decks were built on a sound stage, and the completed film was done so inexpensively that five other similar films could have been produced and still not have equaled the budget on *Bounty*. Never mind that realism was minimized and that, by comparison to *Bounty*, it looked as cheap as it was, with costumes from at least three different centuries and battle scenes clipped from two silent films (*Captain Blood*, 1923, and *The Sea Hawk*, 1924) and inserted between shots of the miniatures in the tank. Still, audiences loved Flynn, De Havilland and the movie. It was first-class popcorn-and-candy, Saturday-matinee fun.

Errol Flynn, Basil Rathbone and Yola D'Avril

Olivia de Havilland and Errol Flynn, one of the public's favorite love teams

70

J. Carrol Naish, Basil Rathbone, Errol Flynn, Guy Kibbee, Ross Alexander and Robert Barrat

Errol Flynn as Dr. Peter Blood and Basil Rathbone as Captain Levasseur crossing swords

Fredric March (1897–1975)

Fredric March entered the acting world in New York with bit parts on stage and extra jobs in films. His role as John Barrymore in a West Coast stage production of *The Royal Family* led to his Hollywood film debut in *The Dummy*, 1929, and 16 other film roles before *Dr. Jekyll and Mr. Hyde*, 1931, his first film of real consequence. March's portrayal of the changeable doctor and his alter ego was impressive and won him the first of his two best-actor Oscars.

Between 1932 and 1934 March appeared in 13 more films, including *Strangers in Love,* 1932, *Design for Living,* 1933 (see page 52), and *The Barretts of Wimpole Street,* 1934. March's favorite of this period was *Death Takes a Holiday,* 1934.

In the mid-30s March appeared in a flock of costume dramas. He was excellent as Jean Valjean in *Les Miserables*, 1935; so-so playing Count Vronsky to Garbo's *Anna Karenina*, 1935; stiff as the title character in *Anthony Adverse*, 1936; and unbelievable as Bothwell in *Mary of Scotland*, 1936 (appearing with his wife, Florence Eldridge). By this time March was rigidly typecast in costume drama and was determined to break from the mold. He did, with his moving portrayal of the fast-fading star in *A Star Is Born*, 1937, with Janet Gaynor. He followed *Star* with the comedy *Nothing Sacred*, 1937.

After making the box-office success *The Buccaneer*, 1938, March and his wife went to New York and for the remainder of the decade alternated between Broadway and Hollywood, where he made two pictures—*There Goes My Heart*, 1938, and *Trade Winds*, 1939. Great things awaited March in the Hollywood of the 40s.

Merrily We Go to Hell *(1932, Paramount) with Sylvia Sydney*

Dr. Jekyll and Mr. Hyde *(1931, Paramount)*

Les Miserables *(1935, United Artists, 20th Century)*

The Sign of the Cross *(1932, Paramount) with Elissa Landi*

Ann Harding (1902–   )

Like Constance Bennett's, Ann Harding's screen career reached its high and low points during the 30s. She was already well known as a Broadway actress when she made her Hollywood debut opposite Fredric March in *Paris Bound,* 1929. She soon became one of the more important stars of the early talking pictures and won an Oscar nomination for her fourth film, Philip Barry's *Holiday,* 1930. She did not try to achieve her recognition with a glamour image but rather used her warm and genteel talent to tug at the heart strings in sudsy sagas like *Her Private Affair,* 1929, and *Gallant Lady,* 1933, and her elegant, sophisticated comedy touch to tickle the funnybone in *Double Harness,* 1933, and *When Ladies Meet,* 1933. Just three years after her debut, her popularity and prestige were such that *The Animal Kingdom,* in which she starred, was chosen to open the Roxy Theatre in New York.

Although Harding received only one Oscar nomination, she gave many performances of Oscar-winning caliber, such as the romantic heroine, Mary, Duchess of Towers, in the haunting poetic fantasy *Peter Ibbetson,* 1935. This film marked the peak of her career. The scripts that followed were ill-chosen and seriously damaged her image. In 1937, no longer sought by the major studios, she went to London to perform in the West End. Returning to Hollywood in 1942, she found that the film industry was not awaiting her with open arms. She was offered parts only in B pictures; her star had faded.

The Fountain *(1934, RKO) with Paul Lukas*

Prestige *(1932, RKO) with Adolphe Menjou and Melvyn Douglas*

Peter Ibbetson *(1935, Paramount) with Gary Cooper*

73

Alfred Hitchcock (1899–   )

As early as 1926, when Hitchcock filmed *The Lodger* as a British silent, the shape of future Hitchcock films was evident—action, with growing tension building up to almost unbearable suspense. In the 30s he made three of his finest films, all in England. They were *The Man Who Knew Too Much,* 1934, with Leslie Banks and Edna Best; *The 39 Steps,* 1935, in which Robert Donat and Madeleine Carroll traverse endless Scottish moors to frustrate an espionage plot, only to find themselves sheltered in the castle of their archenemy; and *The Lady Vanishes,* 1938, an unforgettable thriller in which Miss Froy (Dame May Whitty) is on a train one minute and, unaccountably, gone the next. This last film led *The New York Times* to praise him as England's foremost director and earned him the 1938 New York Film Critics Award for best direction.

After a taut and thrill-packed screen version of Daphne du Maurier's *Jamaica Inn,* 1939, he no longer resisted Hollywood's ardent wooing. David Selznick brought him to the United States, where he promptly won best-picture honors for his first American production, *Rebecca,* 1940.

In later years Hitchcock had his films so carefully preplanned that he is said to have directed from the back seat of his limousine. His portly middle, topped by a solemn moon face relieved only by a slyly twinkling eye, is familiar to millions of moviegoers, who since his first films have watched the screen to spot the Hitchcock trademark—a momentary glimpse of the great man himself somewhere in the background.

The 39 Steps *(1935, Gaumont-British) with Madeleine Carroll and Robert Donat*

The Lady Vanishes *(1938, Gaumont-British) with Mary Clare and Paul Lukas*

The Lady Vanishes*(1938, Gaumont-British) with Michael Redgrave, Margaret Lockwood and Dame May Witty*

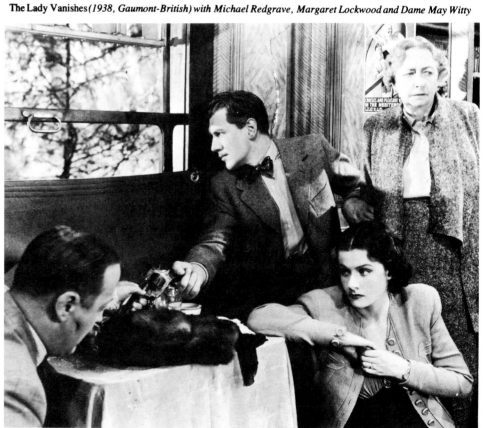

74

The Informer (1935)

John Ford's film about treachery within the resistance movement in Ireland in 1922 was an unusually grim subject for 30s audiences. The studio knew well that the help of critics— often adversaries of the Hollywood moguls—would be necessary, and to catch their attention it ran this prescient message on its ads: "A Prediction: RKO-Radio is convinced that every critic in America will place it on his list of the Ten Best Pictures for 1935." They uniformly did, and thereby the film became a commercial success.

Based on Liam O'Flaherty's novel, the movie realistically creates the shadowy streets and pubs of Dublin, complete with swirling white fog. In the telescoped style of Greek drama the audience is witness to the final twelve hours of revolutionary-turned-informer Gypo Nolan. From his crime Ford constructs a masterful psychological study of guilt and fear. After betraying his best friend for a 20-pound note, Nolan, brilliantly played by Victor McLaglen, moves rapidly from self-confident cunning to panic and remorse. To purge both conscience and fear he takes flight in an orgy of brawling and drinking, as if buying rounds for everyone with the blood money will erase his act. Pursued and hounded by his self-torment, he unwittingly reveals himself as his comrades seek to identify the traitor. His ignominious execution by his peers emphasizes the loneliness of the traitor's path and the tragic implacability of revolutionary justice.

The film earned Ford his first Academy Award for best direction and, perhaps more importantly, his first recognition from critics. McLaglen's portrait of the bullying but cowardly giant won him the year's best-actor designation. Oscars also went to Max Steiner for the musical score and to Dudley Nichols for his screenplay.

Victor McLaglen and Margot Grahame

Victor McLaglen, Joseph Sawyer, Preston Foster and Heather Angel

Victor McLaglen, J. M. Kerrigan and members of the Resistance

Mammy *(1930, Warner Brothers) with music lover and Al Jolson*

The Merry Widow *(1934, M-G-M) with Maurice Chevalier and Jeanette MacDonald*

Musicals

It was with Al Jolson's "Mammy" in *The Jazz Singer*, 1927, that the screen musical was born. In the next three years studios produced blockbusters like M-G-M's *Broadway Melody,* 1929 (the first musical to win the best-picture Oscar), and proclaimed the bill of fare as "100% All Talking * All Singing * All Dancing!" Many new singing stars came to prominence—Nancy Carroll, Jeanette MacDonald, Maurice Chevalier and Helen Kane—while others—Gloria Swanson, Ramon Novarro, Janet Gaynor and Charles Farrell—who had specialized in dramatic parts, were required to prove their singing capabilities.

Every studio plunged into making musicals. Warner Brothers did *My Man*, 1928, *The Singing Fool,* 1928, *Sally*, 1929, *Gold Diggers of Broadway*, 1929, *Mammy*, 1930, and *Sunny*, 1930. M-G-M did *Hollywood Revue*, 1929, using all its top stars whether they could sing or not (Marie Dressler did an underwater ballet spoof), and in 1930 brought Grace Moore to the screen in *Jenny Lind*. Fox made a series of Janet Gaynor–Charles Farrell musicals, including *Sunny Side Up*, 1929, and introduced Sue Carol as a singer and dancer in *Fox Movietone Follies*, 1929. Universal dressed up the melodrama *Broadway*, 1929, with a big dancing finale and starred Paul Whiteman and band in *The King of Jazz*, 1930. Paramount starred Helen Morgan in *Applause*, 1929, and cast cute, sensitive Nancy Carroll in a series of musicals with titles like *Sweetie*, 1929, *Illusion*, 1929, and *Honey*, 1930. Columbia did *Song of Love*, 1929, and Samuel Goldwyn Productions (United Artists) released *Whoopie*, 1930, starring Eddie Cantor.

By 1932 the overexposed musical had lost much of its popularity, but a big revival was just around the corner. (See pages 94-95.)

One Night of Love *(1934, Columbia) with Grace Moore*

Broadway Melody of 1938 *(1937, M-G-M) with Igor Gorin, Sophie Tucker, George Murphy, Eleanor Powell, Robert Taylor, Judy Garland and Buddy Ebsen*

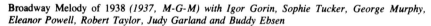

Everybody Sing *(1938, M-G-M) with Judy Garland and Fanny Brice*

Mutiny on the Bounty (1935)

Directed by Frank Lloyd and powerfully acted by Charles Laughton, Clark Gable and Franchot Tone, the film presents the mounting tension between the sadistic, duty-obsessed Captain Bligh (Laughton) and his abused, finally rebellious crew, led by the heroic and dignified first mate, Fletcher Christian (Gable).

The film is based on the first two volumes of a 1932 best seller, *The Bounty Trilogy*, which in turn was drawn from an actual mutiny aboard the H.M.S. *Bounty* in the South Seas two centuries earlier. Yet the film departs from the true event with a romanticized account of the mutineers cavorting with Tahitian native women and distorts the record by sentencing Bligh to the contempt of his fellow officers at the court-martial, when in fact the benevolent British Navy promoted him to the rank of admiral.

But no matter; the film hardly suffers as drama. Laughton's stunning performance as the *Bounty*'s reigning despot makes the viewer shudder with each lash of his relentless whip. After being cast adrift from the *Bounty*, he resolutely guides his small open boat and few loyal men on an astounding 3,000-mile voyage. It is a tribute to the actor that in his new situation he can communicate a heroic image and an indomitable will to survive that moves the formerly hostile audience to admiration.

Gable had reportedly resisted doing *Mutiny on the Bounty* because it was a costume film. But he was excellent in the role of the mutiny's reluctant leader.

Filmed in a large tank on the M-G-M set and "on location" at Catalina Island twenty miles off Los Angeles, the movie won best-picture honors. Its great success for years sparked a wave of sea films.

Franchot Tone as Roger Byam and Clark Gable as Fletcher Christian

Clark Gable, appearing for the last time without a mustache

Dudley Digges, Ian Wolfe, Charles Laughton and Clark Gable

Movita, Clark Gable, Franchot Tone
and Mamo Clark

Charles Laughton as Captain Bligh, facing the mutineers

Douglas Fairbanks, Jr., a streamlined version of his swashbuckling father, in Prisoner of Zenda *(1937)*

One of the earliest and most beautiful shots of Garbo from Camille *(1936)*

Camille (1937)

It was not an unusual role for Garbo—a Parisian courtesan who falls in love only to die tragically of tuberculosis—and she played it in grand style, pulling out all the stops. She was eloquent, lyrical, yet restrained. Her unique poise elevated the story above the level of melodrama and brought her first Oscar nomination. The New York Film Critics gave her their prize as best actress.

Director George Cukor also deserved considerable credit for her heart-rending performance, as well as for that of the young Robert Taylor, who, wearing such heavy make-up that he looked almost as pretty as Garbo, gave one of the more interesting performances of his early career.

Based on Alexandre Dumas' play, *Camille* is the not very original story of the star-crossed love of Marguerite Gautier, a beautiful young courtesan, and socially prominent Armand Duval. Beneath a flirtatious façade she hides a passionate love for him; he loves her madly and is willing to sacrifice wealth, station and career. Armand's father points out to Camille that she will ruin his son's life, and she sacrifices all by deliberately creating an estrangement. When he belatedly realizes what she has done for him he returns to find her dying. Their final embrace is one of the more poignant moments in the film as she draws her final breath and calls, "Armand . . . Armand . . . Arman . . ."

Greta Garbo and Robert Taylor

Robert Taylor, Greta Garbo, Laura Hope Crews and Rex O'Malley

Robert Taylor offering Greta Garbo her favorite flowers, camellias

Greta Garbo as Marguerite Gautier (Camille) and Robert Taylor as Armand

Robert Taylor and Greta Garbo in one of the tender love scenes

83

Robert Taylor and Jessie Ralph with the dying Greta Garbo

Carole Lombard, gracious, witty and lovely to look at

Bette Davis, *the lady of a thousand faces, in a come-hither mood*

Fred Astaire (1899–) and Ginger Rogers (1911–)

During the 20s Fred Astaire and his sister Adele were the dancing darlings of Broadway. Then Adele married and retired, and in 1933 Fred went to Hollywood. M-G-M matched Fred with Joan Crawford in *Dancing Lady*. It was something less than a triumph for all concerned.

Meanwhile, pert and sexy Ginger Rogers, also Broadway-trained, had created a considerable stir with a single screen line—"Cigarette me, Big Boy"—in *Young Man of Manhattan*, 1930. By the time she played the chorus girl in Warners' *42nd Street*, 1933, she was popular in her own right.

The heaven-made movie duo of Astaire and Rogers began when RKO starred Dolores Del Rio and Gene Raymond in *Flying Down to Rio*, 1933. The Carioca, as danced by Fred and Ginger, stole the show. Until the end of the 30s the team danced together, becoming the best-known terpsichorean couple of their era. Astaire was a perfectionist, inventive, engaging and mercilessly hard-working. Ginger was a quick study, with almost equal dedication. On screen together they sparkled.

The Gay Divorcee, 1934, in which they demonstrated the Continental, was followed by *Roberta*, 1935. *Top Hat*, 1935, had them dancing "Cheek to Cheek," and *Follow the Fleet*, 1936, featured "Let's Face the Music and Dance." In the 30s there were eight Astaire–Rogers vehicles. By 1939, however, the magic was fading or perhaps the public was getting just a bit jaded. In any event, their last picture together was *The Story of Vernon and Irene Castle,* 1939. Astaire's contract with RKO ended, and he went on to dance with other ladies, notably Rita Hayworth, Judy Garland and Cyd Charisse. As for Miss Rogers, she promptly won the 1940 Academy Award as best actress of the year in the non-dancing, non-singing *Kitty Foyle*.

Swing Time (1936, RKO)

The Story of Vernon and Irene Castle (1939, RKO)

The Gay Divorcee *(1934, RKO)*

Swing Time *(1936, RKO)*

Look

10¢

March 15, 1938

FLASH GORDON
Goes to Mars!
A Fantastic New Movie Serial—Page 59

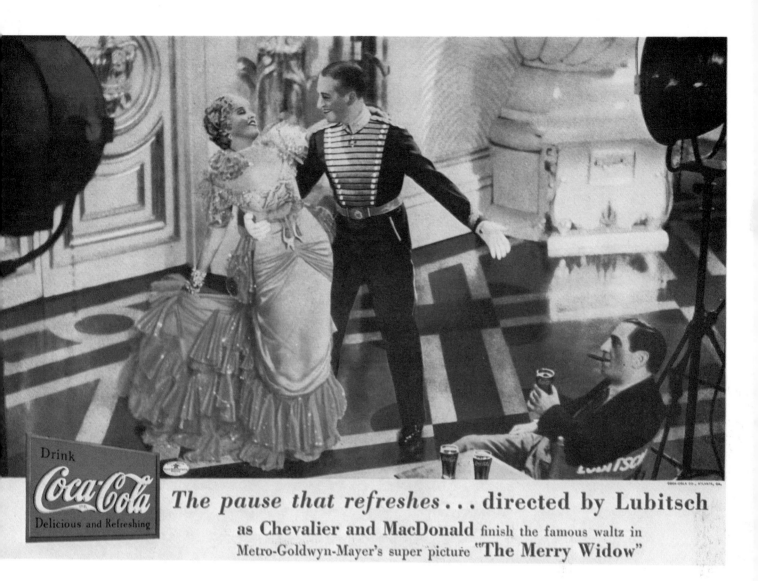

The pause that refreshes... directed by Lubitsch as Chevalier and MacDonald finish the famous waltz in Metro-Goldwyn-Mayer's super picture "The Merry Widow"

Drink Coca-Cola
Delicious and Refreshing

The talkies were an endless source of material for big-time advertisers in the 30s. The Coca-Cola spread above features the Good Housekeeping seal of approval and Ernst Lubitsch, who appears to be filtering his Coke through a cigar. Dancing daintily about, Jeanette MacDonald and Maurice Chevalier permit their Cokes on the table to lose their fizz. Though both Chevalier and MacDonald have left us, Jeanette's now camp voice lives on.

OPPOSITE *Here nostalgia reigns supreme. Look is no more. Ten-cent magazines are a thing of the past. Flash Gordon portrayed by the muscular Buster Crabbe is no longer with us. Only the lady in distress with her bare midriff and ankle-strap shoes has a Today appearance.*

The Girl of the Golden West *(1938, M-G-M)*

Jeanette MacDonald (1901–1965)
and Nelson Eddy (1901–1967)

M-G-M's "Singing Sweethearts," warbling nose to nose in wildly improbable romantic comedies, were two of the most popular musical stars of the mid-to-late 30s. The reddish-haired MacDonald came to Hollywood via Broadway and made her film debut opposite Maurice Chevalier in the popular film *The Love Parade,* 1929. Between her debut and her first co-starring role with Eddy in *Naughty Marietta,* 1935, she made six films, three with Chevalier, and established herself as a winning leading lady.

Eddy had made a name for himself as a successful concert singer when he was discovered by an M-G-M scout and cast in a small role in *Broadway to Hollywood,* 1933. He appeared briefly in two other films before being cast opposite MacDonald in *Naughty Marietta.* Audiences were enthusiastic over the singing lovers, and M-G-M rushed to create other vehicles for them.

Though MacDonald and Eddy were given co-star billing, it was she who dominated their films. In their best, *Maytime,* 1937, she was seldom off screen, while Eddy managed to appear for approximately 30 of the film's 136 minutes. In *Rose Marie,* 1936, and *Girl of the Golden West,* 1938, even the titles emphasized MacDonald's end of the act. Both presences were indicated by *Sweethearts,* 1939, but there again it was MacDonald who held the spotlight. One critic was heard to cry in desperation, "Getting a look at Eddy is like trying to meet Garbo!"

Nelson Eddy and Jeanette MacDonald made three films together in the 40s and then went their separate ways. Both had seen their heyday, and each had only four more films ahead.

Naughty Marietta *(1935, M-G-M)*

Sweethearts *(1938, M-G-M)*

Maytime *(1937, M-G-M)*

Rose Marie *(1936, M-G-M)*

Clark Gable as Harry ''Personality'' Van, a vaudeville hoofer of the six-a-day era, was at the top of his form in the 1939 film version of Idiot's Delight, *Robert Sherwood's Pulitzer Prize-winning play about Europe on the brink of war. The sextet of glamour girls, in no special order, are Virginia Gray, Paula Stone, Joan Marsh, Virginia Dale, Lorraine Krueger and Bernadene Hayes. Norma Shearer was the co-star, and Clarence Brown directed.*

OPPOSITE *For the information of those who have never seen a motion picture, here is the one and only W. C. Fields, indulging in his favorite indoor and outdoor sport.*

100 Men and a Girl *(1937, Universal) with Deanna Durbin and Leopold Stokowski*

Musicals

After the public's taste for musicals had been sated by the productions of the late 20s and early 30s, Warner Brothers, the company that had introduced sound to films with *The Jazz Singer*, 1927, repopularized the musical genre with *42nd Street*, 1933. With a plot built around the backstage hysteria attending the show-must-go-on philosophy, stars like Warner Baxter, Ruby Keeler, George Brent, Bebe Daniels, Ginger Rogers and Dick Powell and the kaleidoscopic production numbers staged by Busby Berkeley, it was a sure-fire success. Audience response was so enthusiastic that a second, almost identical, film was rushed into release, *Footlight Parade*, 1933, with a slightly altered cast. James Cagney demonstrated his singing and tap-dancing skills in ''Shanghai Lil,'' Dick Powell and Ruby Keeler sang ''By a Waterfall'' and ''Honeymoon Hotel,'' and Joan Blondell provided wisecracks. At least ten other Warner musicals, including *Gold Diggers of 1933*, *Dames*, 1934, *Fashions of 1934* and *Gold Diggers of 1935*, were made in a similar mold and saw Mr. Berkeley choreographing such unlikely items as photographs, pianos, rocking chairs and human harps.

Once again, the other studios jumped on the bandwagon. RKO-Radio Pictures combined the sensational Fred Astaire and Ginger Rogers (see pages 86–87). M-G-M scored a rousing success with the Oscar-winning *The Great Ziegfeld* (see pages 98–99), 1936, and struck a box-office gold mine with the singing duo of Jeanette MacDonald and Nelson Eddy (see page 90). Fox studios was saved from bankruptcy when six-year-old Shirley Temple captured America's heart by singing and dancing in *Stand Up and Cheer* and *Baby Takes a Bow*, both in 1934. Walt Disney created one of the most beautiful musicals of the decade, *Snow White and the Seven Dwarfs*, 1937, in which cartoon characters danced to and sang 11 songs, including the unforgettable ''Some Day My Prince Will Come,'' ''Heigh-Ho'' and ''Whistle While You Work.''

There were many other stars of this genre: Eleanor Powell, Alice Faye, Eddie Cantor, Deanna Durbin, Sonja Henie, Judy Garland, Mickey Rooney and Bing Crosby. The musical, as it had been transformed in the 30s, had a long life ahead of it.

Thin Ice *(1937, 20th Century–Fox) with Sonja Henie*

Going Hollywood *(1933, M-G-M) with Bing Crosby and Marion Davies*

Broadway Melody of 1938 *(1937, M-G-M) with Eleanor Powell*

Gold Diggers of 1933 *(1933, Warner Brothers)* with Ruby Keeler

42nd Street *(1933, Warner Brothers)*

Little Shirley has grown a lot, almost enough to bring her film career as a prestigious toddler to an end.

Shirley Temple (1928–)

The precocious dimpled daughter of a Santa Monica bank manager got her start in movies in a series of shorts entitled "Baby Burlesks," and before she reached the age of six she was hired to sing one song, "Baby Take a Bow," for Fox's *Stand Up and Cheer*, 1934. The song never became as famous as "On the Good Ship Lollipop" in her later 1934 film *Bright Eyes*, but it launched the child star on a truly phenomenal screen career. For the next four years Shirley Temple was the world's number-one box-office attraction. Her salary rocketed to $100,000 per film by 1938 (it had been $150 a week when she signed with Fox).

Prompted by her remarkable stardom, hordes of mothers barged into the offices of producers and talent agents with curly-haired moppets they insisted were "another Shirley Temple." But she was one of a kind. She was not just a chubby-cheeked tot whose hair had been done up in ringlets but a performer with amazing talent. When she sang it was as if an adult were imitating a child, and her tap dancing all but upstaged top-flight hoofers like Bill "Bojangles" Robinson and Buddy Ebsen. The energy and enthusiasm of her acting bordered more on caricature than characterization; still, she seduced audiences into her innocent, make-believe world where a child could help an ex-convict father go straight (*Baby Take a Bow*, 1934), bring estranged parents back together (*Now and Forever*, 1934) or tell Abraham Lincoln he was "almost nice enough to be a Confederate" (*The Littlest Rebel*, 1935).

When, in *Heidi*, 1937, the future U. S. Ambassador knelt and prayed, "Dear God, please make every little boy and girl in the world as happy as I am," audiences all over the world could have sighed an almost audible "Amen."

She became the definitive *Rebecca of Sunnybrook Farm*, 1938, and was appropriately regal in *The Little Princess*, 1939, but she began to fail at the box office, and her popularity continued to wane during the 40s.

Heidi *(1937, 20th Century–Fox) with* Jean Hersholt

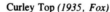

Curley Top *(1935, Fox)*

Shirley Temple *(1935)*

The Little Colonel *(1935, Fox) with Bill "Bojangles" Robinson*

Myrna Loy as Ziegfeld's wife Billie Burke

The Great Ziegfeld (1936)

Here was M-G-M's musical-to-top-all-musicals! It could hardly be otherwise, considering its subject—the extravagant life and loves of Broadway's legendary impresario, Florenz Ziegfeld (William Powell), creator of the *Ziegfeld Follies*. No expense was spared on this three-hour production—it reportedly cost Metro $500,000 an hour—which won best-picture honors for 1936. True to Ziegfeld tradition, it featured extravagant sets and brilliant costumes, but the exuberant, elaborately staged song-and-dance numbers packed the greatest wallop. There were ten smashing production numbers, including a finale, Irving Berlin's "A Pretty Girl Is Like a Melody," that outscaled anything ever seen on the musical screen.

For a performance requiring little more than pantomiming lyrics, looking soulful, and talking into the telephone, Luise Rainer was named the year's best actress. As Anna Held, Ziegfeld's first wife, Miss Rainer allegedly clinched the Oscar for one particular sequence, a telephone conversation with Ziegfeld in which she congratulates him on his marriage to Billie Burke (Myrna Loy). "Sounds fonny," she intones in her Viennese accent, fighting back the tears, "an ex-hozban an' wife, telling each ozah how happy they are, *oui*?" The following year she again reaped the best-actress award (for *The Good Earth*, 1937), becoming the first consecutive winner in the history of the motion-picture academy.

With the advent of color, later musicals surpassed *The Great Ziegfeld*, but in the 30s it was the most lavish and magnificent of its kind and provided a model for successors.

William Powell as Flo Ziegfeld and Luise Rainer as Anna Held

William Powell in title role

98

OPPOSITE *"A Pretty Girl Is Like a Melody" finale*

Clark Gable and Jeanette MacDonald

The beginning of the earthquake that would destroy the city of San Francisco

San Francisco (1936)

Director W. S. Van Dyke took an Anita Loos screenplay, three magnetic and exciting stars (Clark Gable, Jeanette MacDonald and Spencer Tracy), added a spectacular ten-minute earthquake and created one of the 30s' most thoroughly entertaining features. One might wonder if the film-makers had intended the film to be symbolic as well, with the earthquake representing the Depression and MacDonald as the free, longing spirit of the nation.

The story begins in 1905. Mary (MacDonald), goodhearted and decent, is a singer in the Barbary Coast honky-tonk café owned by the opportunistic, amoral Blackie (Gable). The disparate couple fall in love and immediately run into trouble. His old pal Tim (Tracy), now a priest, tries to help them, but Blackie is impossible. Father Tim throws his hands up in despair, Mary breaks her singing contract with the saloon and becomes an opera singer, the toast of San Francisco's Nob Hill elite.

It's 1906, Blackie is down on his luck and Mary nobly tries to help out by representing his saloon in the city's annual talent contest. She delivers a rousing rendition of ''San Francisco'' and wins, only to be publicly rebuked and humiliated by Gable. He storms off, she cries and the earthquake hits. The ground opens up, fires rage, buildings fall into the street, crowds are buried under rubble and Blackie realizes he has made a terrible mistake. He stumbles through the ruins looking frantically for Mary. Finally, in the company of all-forgiving Father Tim, he finds her standing on a hilltop singing. He repents his wicked ways, they embrace and arm in arm lead hundreds of survivors back into the city to begin reconstruction. *San Francisco* was, and still is, despite the schmaltz, dynamite!

Jeanette MacDonald as Mary Blake, comforting the earthquake victims

Spencer Tracy as Father Tim Mullen and Clark Gable as Blackie Norton

Spencer Tracy, Warren Hymer and Clark Gable

Jean Arthur and John Miljan, who played General Custer

The Plainsman (1936)

Direct from their co-starring triumph in *Mr. Deeds Goes to Town*, 1936, Gary Cooper and Jean Arthur were signed by Cecil B. De Mille to play the salty frontier characters Wild Bill Hickok and Calamity Jane in his big-scale view of western America during and following the Civil War. Seldom before had De Mille achieved such a high level of artistry. From Cooper and Arthur he got delightful, individual characterizations as they struggled through hair-raising adventures and an on-again, off-again romance. Cooper's strong, silent, dedicated Hickok was beautifully counterpointed by Arthur's willful, bubbly, gutsy and winning Jane. The script was particularly literate, and for the first time De Mille paid attention to the natural "silences" of life. He wisely kept the focus on his stars, although still working with countless numbers of extras in whose ranks were Anthony Quinn and Victor Varconi (playing Indians), John Miljan, George Cleveland, George "Gabby" Hayes, Fuzzy Knight and Bud Flanagan (Dennis O'Keefe).

Because *The Plainsman* was obviously intended as "family fare," the censors insisted that some pruning be done on the sequence in which Cooper is tied by his hands to a wooden spit and lowered into a flaming pit by Indians trying to elicit information about the position of Custer's troops. The censors contended this extreme and excessive torture was best left to the imagination. In the released version, however, this sequence was still grisly and gave the film one of its most suspenseful moments. As pure escapist entertainment *The Plainsman* ranks with the best Westerns produced during the 30s.

Gary Cooper and Jean Arthur in one of their few tender moments

Porter Hall, Gary Cooper, Jean Arthur, Ted Oliver and Fred Kohler, Sr.

Jean Arthur as Calamity Jane and Gary Cooper as Wild Bill Hickok

Victor Varconi, Paul Harvey, Gary Cooper and Jean Arthur

Censored torture scene; it was considered too explicit

Gary Cooper (1901–1961)

Fighting Caravans *(1931, Paramount) with Lily Damita*

Mr. Deeds Goes to Town *(1936, Columbia) with Jean Arthur*

The Cowboy and the Lady *(1938, United Artists, Samuel Goldwyn) with Merle Oberon*

Conjecture has always surrounded the mysterious chemistry between actor and camera which makes for ''star'' magic. Whatever it is, Gary Cooper probably had more of it than any other actor in screen history. His presence dominated all of the films in which he starred. Tall, lanky, handsome—at times almost pretty but not effeminate—graceful with a self-conscious suggestion of awkwardness, he could suggest great vulnerability without appearing weak and communicate volumes with a simple ''yup.'' No other actor could have more perfectly represented Hemingway's heroic soldier in *A Farewell to Arms*, 1932, or the precocious country boy in *Mr. Deeds Goes to Town*, 1936. He personified romance in *Peter Ibbetsen*, 1935, courage in *The Real Glory*, 1939, genuine innocence in *Desire*, 1936.

After riding horses as an extra in several dusty Westerns, he got his first break with a small role in *The Winning of Barbara Worth*, 1926, which led to a Paramount contract. He was cast opposite Clara Bow in *It*, 1927, and the ''It Girl,'' having fallen in love with him, demanded he get the lead male role in her *Children of Divorce*, 1927. But it was the starring role in *The Virginian*, 1929, his first talkie, that rocketed him to fame and top billing. He made 27 films between 1926 and 1931, but after *I Take This Woman* he was ill and exhausted, and he fled to Europe.

From Europe he went to Africa on a safari, where word reached him that Paramount was pushing a new star, Cary Grant, to scare him about his future. The tactic worked, and Cooper returned to America with new determination to work at his profession. His best films in this period were *A Farewell to Arms*, directed by Frank Borzage, and *Design for Living*, 1933, directed by Ernst Lubitsch. After a number of routine features he emerged as an actor without equal in such hits as *Lives of a Bengal Lancer*, 1935, and *Mr. Deeds* (which he made on loan to Frank Capra at Columbia). Except for this last film, his scripts were not worthy of his enormous talents, and he waited until 1942 to receive the first of his two Oscars for *Sergeant York* (the other was for *High Noon*, 1952).

Beau Geste *(1939, Paramount) with Robert Preston, Susan Hayward and Ray Milland*

104

A Farewell to Arms *(1932, Paramount) with Helen Hayes*

One Sunday Afternoon *(1933, Paramount) with Frances Fuller*

The Devil and the Deep *(1932, Paramount) with Tallulah Bankhead*

The Adventures of Marco Polo *(1938, United Artists, Samuel Goldwyn) with Sigrid Gurie*

Leslie Howard and Norma Shearer as the young lovers

A secret meeting between Romeo, Leslie Howard, and Juliet, Norma Shearer

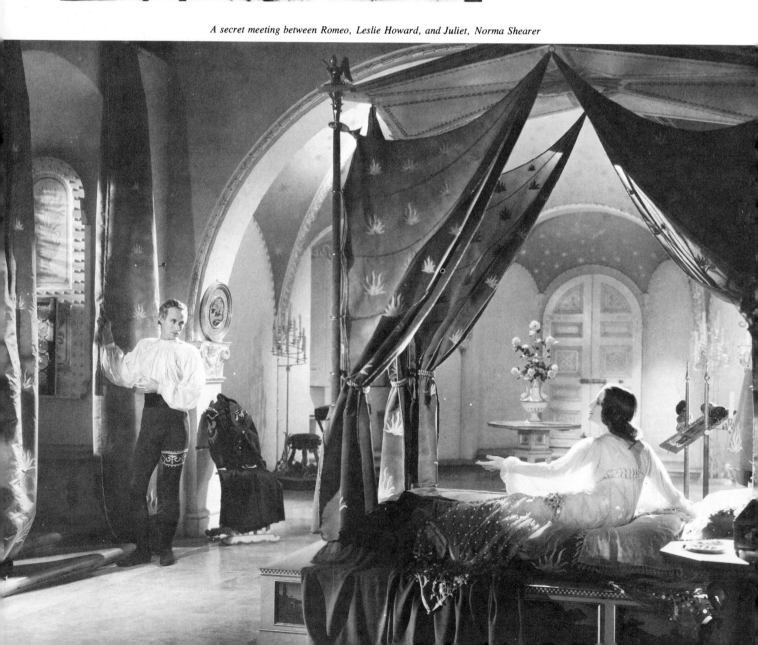

Romeo and Juliet (1936)

When M-G-M's boy wizard, Irving Thalberg, announced his plans to film Hollywood's first sound version of a Shakespearean tragedy no one was really surprised, although an untested box-office commodity was a big gamble. Thalberg had long maintained a reputation for adding an artistic dimension to the dollar-oriented motion-picture industry. What did surprise some people was the casting of Thalberg's 36-year-old wife, Norma Shearer, and 43-year-old Leslie Howard in the roles of the star-crossed, teenaged lovers. However, the deft use of gauze over the camera lens gave both stars an aura of youth and made them believable in their roles.

The film was prepared with great care and was lavishly mounted. Elaborate sets were constructed and stunning costumes were designed. Both Shearer and Howard gave accomplished performances that were praised by the critics. By today's standards, John Barrymore's portrayal of Mercutio was a hammy, self-indulgent performance. However, it was more than compensated for by that of Edna May Oliver, one of the 30s most brilliant character actresses, who gave a delightful, affectionate rendering of Juliet's cantankerous, bossy old nurse.

Shortly after the film's release, Irving Thalberg died at the age of 37, and Miss Shearer retired from the screen until 1938, when she returned to play the title role in *Marie Antoinette* (see pages 132–133), another project she and Thalberg had planned.

Although *Romeo and Juliet* enjoyed a good press and won a best-picture nomination for itself and a best-actress nomination for Shearer (her fifth), the revenues it brought in covered little more than production costs. Thalberg's gamble had not paid off. A Shakespearean tragedy would not prove to be good box-office until *Hamlet*, 1948.

Norma Shearer

Leslie Howard

John Barrymore

Paris, Ralph Forbes, is wounded by Leslie Howard during their duel

Leslie Howard as Alan Squire and Bette Davis as Gabby Maple

The Petrified Forest (1936)

The basic ingredients for dramatic excitement in a stark, barren setting where grim realities and poetic visions clash were present in Robert E. Sherwood's play, but it lacked the depth and humanity that would give it substance. The screen version of *The Petrified Forest* did no more to flesh out the plot than did the original. It amounts to little more than so much pseudo-poetic, semi-sophomoric philosophizing about one remarkably shoddy notion: that a depressed poet and a crazed killer can make a worthwhile contribution to the world. They will do this when the killer shoots the poet, thereby enabling a young woman who fancies herself a painter to cash the poet's insurance policy and go to Paris for training.

Although it has its weaknesses, *The Petrified Forest* is important if only because it brought Humphrey Bogart back to Hollywood to recreate his stage role of Duke Mantee and to establish himself as the number-one villain and tough guy in films. Thirty-five years old, Bogart, with a record of nine so-so films to his credit, was given fifth billing and virtually walked off with the picture despite the efforts of its stars, Leslie Howard and Bette Davis. In fact, it is Bogart and his terrifying, cold-blooded Mantee who salvages the film and invests it with a semblance of reality. Leslie Howard, as the poet who has dropped out of society, simply chalked up another embarrassingly whiny characterization to his screen record of sentimental anti-heroes. And Bette Davis, never lovelier, managed to be less hysterical than usual but was not convincing enough to make many people believe in her artistic aspirations.

Humphrey Bogart, John Alexander, Charles Grapewin, Bette Davis, Leslie Howard, Genevieve Tobin and Paul Harvey

Bette Davis with Humphrey Bogart, who plays the murderous Duke Mantee

Charles Grapewin, Genevieve Tobin, Leslie Howard, Paul Harvey, Bette Davis, Humphrey Bogart and Joseph Sawyer

Charles Laughton (1899–1962)

With his snub nose, thick lips and rotund body, Charles Laughton was a far cry from the traditional image of a movie star. His detractors called him moody, temperamental, unpredictable and maddening to work with. On occasion he was overly dramatic. Nevertheless, he turned in some of the top performances of the 30s.

A series of London stage and screen successes brought him to Broadway and then to Hollywood in the early 30s. In 1932 he made six films, the most outstanding of which was De Mille's *The Sign of the Cross*. Cast as Nero, Laughton drew notice to himself because of his approach to his role. He was wonderfully funny, making satiric jabs at Mussolini, and gave audiences many laughs and studio bosses high blood pressure.

After some so-so efforts he returned to England and under Alexander Korda's direction gave a brilliant performance in *The Private Life of Henry VIII*, 1933. His portrayal of Henry not only won him the best-actor Oscar but also helped to make the film one of the first British pictures to enjoy worldwide acclaim.

Returning to Hollywood, Laughton created some of his most famous characterizations: the tyrannical, possessive father of Elizabeth Barrett Browning in *The Barretts of Wimpole Street*, 1934; the dignified English butler transported to the wild West in *Ruggles of Red Gap*, 1935; and, perhaps best of all, the cruel, inflexible Captain Bligh in *Mutiny on the Bounty*, 1935 (see page 78), for which he won an Academy Award nomination.

After making *Mutiny*, Laughton left Metro and returned to England to make *Rembrandt*, 1936, with Korda. He then helped form a film company and acted in its productions which were, for the most part, unsuccessful. His last film of the 30s was *Jamaica Inn*, 1939. The 40s found him back in Hollywood with more triumphs ahead of him.

The Private Life of Henry VIII *(1933, United Artists, Alexander Korda)*

The Beachcomber *(1938, Paramount) with Robert Newton*

White Woman *(1933, Paramount) with Carole Lombard*

110

Rembrandt *(1936, London Films)*

The Barretts of Wimpole Street *(1934, M-G-M)*

The Sign of the Cross *(1932, Paramount)*

The Beachcomber *(1938, Paramount)*

Anthony Adverse (1936)

This film, adapted from Hervey Allen's best-selling novel, is a compelling union of personal drama and historic pageant. It follows the development of a youth, Anthony Adverse (Fredric March), as he comes of age traveling throughout Europe and America. Adverse's story is shown against the background of nineteenth-century historic events and social conditions.

Director Mervyn LeRoy faced the problem of giving continuity to a film that is episodic and peppered with old-fashioned title cards. He solved the problem beautifully by keeping the pace fast and concentrating on Anthony as a unifying force. The film is one of LeRoy's most competent directing achievements.

Adverse's story is an exciting one and reveals not only the young man's extraordinary adventures but also gives a rather surprising view of the culture and morals of the time. Our hero Adverse is not averse to dealing in the slave trade. His beloved, the lovely Angela (Olivia de Havilland), has love affairs right and left. In the meantime, Napoleon (Rollo Lloyd) is wreaking havoc in Europe and kindly confides to Anthony that conquest is not necessarily an evil way of life.

The film is not profound, but it is entertaining, with lavish costumes, beautiful sets and scenery and an impressive cast, including Anita Louise, Edmund Gwenn, Claude Rains, Louis Haywood, Gale Sondergaard and Akim Tamiroff. *Anthony Adverse* was nominated for the best-picture Oscar and received Academy Awards for cinematography, musical score and editing. Gale Sondergaard won the first supporting-actress award ever given for her brilliant performance as the villainess, Faith.

Akim Tamiroff and Fredric March

Fredric March as title character

Academy Award winner Gale Sondergaard as Faith and Claude Rains as Don Luis

Rollo Lloyd and Olivia de Havilland

112

Fredric March and Olivia de Havilland

Fredric March and Scotty Beckett, who plays his son

Olivia de Havilland as Angela Guisseppi

Luise Rainer as O-lan

The Good Earth (1937)

Everything about this movie was on a grand scale. Filmed on five hundred acres of California terrain that had been converted into a Chinese village and farmland, and utilizing footage taken in China for process shots, it took four years to make and went through two directors and producers. One of M-G-M's "prestige" pictures of the 30s, it was Irving Thalberg's last film (he died shortly after completion of shooting) and the only film for which, on Louis B. Mayer's orders, he got any screen credit.

The film balanced simplicity and grandeur in adapting to the screen Pearl Buck's novel about the devotion of Chinese peasants to their land. The travails of Wang and O-lan are forcefully played by Paul Muni and Luise Rainer. Miss Rainer, as the mistreated but steadfastly loyal slave-bride, won her second Oscar for this performance. If the production had a leisurely pace, it was a technique appropriate to the film's unpretentious Oriental setting.

The picture followed the novel closely but invented a cinematic, dramatic ending that became the movie's best remembered scene and among the most impressive spectacles in film history. A terrifying plague of locusts descends on Wang's crops, threatening to destroy his work and impressing on him that his land is more important than his worldly ambitions. The epic quality of his return to basic values and triumph over nature was heart-warming to millions of Americans of the era. Though audiences were far removed from the life of this Chinese farmer, their struggles amid the Depression were not altogether different. Wang's redemption was a good tonic for those troubled times.

Luise Rainer, Paul Muni and children

Paul Muni, the man of many faces, as Wang

114

Luise Rainer in the role that won her a second Academy Award

Paul Muni and Luise Rainer

Robert Taylor (1911–1969)

Hollywood's most legendary "tall, dark and handsome" matinee idol, Rudolph Valentino, was frequently called "powder puff," "pretty boy" and other equally insinuating appellations. Perhaps because he physically fit the Valentino image, Robert Taylor endured the same absurd tags throughout his early, meteoric rise to stardom. It was the men in the audience who seemed to question his masculinity; the women adored him. After Taylor appeared in a small part in *Society Doctor*, 1935, women wrote thousands of letters weekly, demanding that M-G-M cast him in larger parts. While he was on loan to Universal Pictures for *Magnificent Obsession*, 1935, he was elevated to star status, making the top five in nearly every popularity poll of the year. Interestingly, he played a doctor in both films, his father's profession and one that his family had wanted him to follow.

Taylor was never a bad actor; he just was never really good. His face was obviously his fortune, and he seemed to know it. Of course, there was an occasional embarrassing film such as *Camille*, 1937, in which he appeared so heavily rouged, lipsticked and downright pretty that he and Garbo might just as easily have switched roles. It was in action films like *The Crowd Roars,* 1938, that he appeared most effectively. He was strong, self-composed, entirely capable of holding his own in any man's world. Also, his marriage to Barbara Stanwyck in 1939 helped silence the powder-puff gossip. From then on he specialized in roles that were more of the he-man, tough-guy variety, playing soldiers, gangsters, cowboys regularly during the 40s and 50s and thus becoming popular with the male audience as well.

His Brother's Wife (1936, M-G-M) with Barbara Stanwyck

Magnificent Obsession (1935, Universal) with Irene Dunne

Personal Property (1937, M-G-M) with Jean Harlow

Three Comrades (1938, M-G-M) with Margaret Sullavan, Franchot Tone and Robert Young

116

Jean Harlow (1911–1937)

Hollywood had seen vamps before, but Jean Harlow—the tough-as-nails, tarty sex symbol of the 30s—was a new phenomenon. She had frizzy, flagrantly bottle-blond hair and a supple body that, lasciviously swathed in sheer crepe, radiated the ultimate in sex appeal. But stardom was also based on her brilliant comic playing of vulgar, hard-boiled and wisecracking sirens, female equivalents of the male toughs of the era.

Her private life read like a dime-store novel: married at 16, divorced at 19; married for two months at 21, then widowed when her husband, M-G-M producer Paul Bern, committed suicide; married for the last time at 22 and divorced at 24. Her professional career was more successful but short-lived. After a few bit parts (among them in Chaplin's *City Lights*) she began her ascent to Hollywood's heights with leading roles in Howard Hughes's *Hell's Angels*, 1930, and William Wellman's *The Public Enemy*, 1931. The combination of *Goldie* and *Platinum Blonde*, both 1931, sealed her screen image. In the former the word *tramp* first entered the screen's vocabulary; Frank Capra's *Platinum Blonde* contributed her nickname.

She was by now big at the box office, but she was still in the doghouse with critics. Hughes passed her contract to M-G-M for a cool $60,000, and under Metro's careful training and casting she developed into a fine comedienne. She darkened her hair for *Red Headed Woman*, 1932, but was platinum again in *Red Dust*, playing a floozie opposite Clark Gable. Their brawling romance ignited the screen with its earthy sexiness (*Time* magazine referred to the film's "brazen moral values") and endeared Harlow to critics and popular audiences alike. She and Gable returned in *Hold Your Man*, 1933, *China Seas*, 1935, *Wife vs. Secretary*, 1936, and *Saratoga*, 1937, during the filming of which she died at the age of 26, reportedly from uremic poisoning.

Saratoga *(1937, M-G-M) with Clark Gable*

Suzy *(1936, M-G-M) with Cary Grant*

Reckless *(1935, M-G-M) with William Powell, Rosalind Russell and guests*

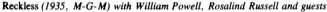

Riffraff *(1936, M-G-M) with Spencer Tracy*

Claire Trevor as Francie, Baby Face Martin's girl

Dead End (1937)

Part of the story of *Dead End* is told by the environment in which the action takes place—the dead-end tenement streets bordering on the posh sections of Manhattan's East Side. Though the film version of Sidney Kingsley's play was not shot on location, it has the flavor of hopelessness, decay and poverty that characterized such tenement blocks.

Dead End begins with the return of gangster Baby Face Martin (Humphrey Bogart). He returns to the tenements to see his mother and his old girlfriend and to hide from the law. He is not the story's center, however, but rather serves as an example of how poverty breeds crime and how crime produces more crime. Martin's tough allure, his silk shirts and easy money glorify wrongdoing in the eyes of the deprived youths of the tenements. Much of the action centers around the efforts of Dave (Joel McCrea) to stop Martin from attracting six adolescent toughies to a life of crime. (The six later became known as the "Dead End Kids.")

The constant use of contrast between rich and poor involves the audience to the point where one can almost forgive Bogart his life of crime (how else is one to raise himself up from such abject poverty?). The film makes it very clear in the end, however, that crime does not pay and that decent people can survive. Bogart's mother (Marjorie Main) sends him away with a slap and an order to "stay away . . . and die." He does, in the gutter, shot by McCrea.

The success of this engrossing, if depressing, film surprised many. Its grim picture of tenement life and its controversial social elements did not seem the fare for 30s audiences. But audiences did go to see *Dead End*, and, as a result, a new film genre, the social drama, developed.

Sylvia Sidney, Robert F. Homans, Billy Halop, Bernard Punsley, Bobby Jordan and Huntz Hall

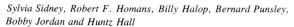

Joel McCrea as Dave and Sylvia Sidney as Drina

118

Spencer Tracy (1900–1967)

He may not have had the glamour of Gable, the good looks of Cooper or the dynamism of Cagney or Bogart, yet Spencer Tracy was one of the most "natural" actors ever to grace the screen. His technique was simple: "Just know your lines and don't bump into the furniture," he said. Tracy did that all right, but there was no part that he couldn't handle effortlessly—gangster, priest, soldier or sailor, Presidential candidate, irate father—he was consistently natural, consistently brilliant.

His first films, beginning with *Up the River*, 1930, were mainly grade-B gangster pictures, and it wasn't until *20,000 Years in Sing Sing*, 1933, when he replaced James Cagney (who was feuding with his studio), that he became widely known. Several films followed in rapid succession, some of them mediocre in spite of Tracy's uniformly good performances. Executives at Fox, his studio, knew he was very good, but displeased by his unruliness and convinced he lacked sex appeal, they weren't too upset when he moved over to Metro in 1935.

The 12 pictures Tracy made for M-G-M in the last half of the 30s brought him the first few of his nine Academy Award nominations, a record still unbroken by any male actor, and two Oscars as best actor of the year. *Riff Raff*, 1936, with Jean Harlow, was a promising beginning, but top stardom came with Fritz Lang's *Fury*, 1936; the big-budgeted *San Francisco*, 1936, in which he played a priest locked in battle with his saloon-proprietor friend Clark Gable; *Captains Courageous*, 1937, which yielded his first Oscar; *Test Pilot*, 1938, again with Gable; and *Boys Town*, 1938, wherein he earned Oscar number two—in consecutive years, a record for a male star—as the crusading Father Flanagan.

As the 30s ended Tracy was at his peak. He was passing Gable in popularity polls and was soon to begin making pictures with Katharine Hepburn. In his book on Tracy and Hepburn, Garson Kanin described the stalwart actor as operating on "a plateau beyond greatness."

They Gave Him a Gun *(1937, M-G-M)*

Up the River *(1930, Fox) with Humphrey Bogart*

Boys Town *(1938, M-G-M) with Mickey Rooney*

Letty Lynton *(1932, M-G-M) with Nils Asther*

Joan Crawford (1904–)

Already established as one of M-G-M's most important stars in silent pictures, Joan Crawford had little difficulty reaching even greater popularity in talking pictures. In the 20s she had epitomized the flapper, and throughout the 30s she represented a glamourized, more sophistocated version of the all-American woman—hard-working, courageous, often down but never defeated. Her characters were usually girls from the wrong side of the tracks who leave home, go to work and end up stylishly installed in a lushly furnished flat.

As a personality she was even more compelling than as an actress. Articulate and candid in interviews, she expounded the "Crawford Philosophy" on everything from success, fashion and menus to marriage, children and divorce. Primarily, however, she talked about Joan Crawford. She was considered "hot" copy, with more written about her than any other star. Only one of her films of the 30s revealed her considerable acting talents—*Grand Hotel*, 1932. Her stenographer-on-the-make, Flaemmchen, was such a snappy, multifaceted performance that she virtually eclipsed the prestigious Garbo, John Barrymore and Wallace Beery. (See page 38.) With the exception of this role, she relied on her remarkable face, large dark eyes, high cheekbones and magnificently proportioned figure to attract attention. Hers was such an imposing image that there was only one male star who could complement her on screen: Clark Gable. In their five films together during the 30s they represented the screen's most handsome, formidable duo. Not until 1939, when she wisely asked to play the gold-digging Crystal Allen in *The Women*, did the Crawford of *Grand Hotel* re-emerge. It marked the rebirth of an actress and prepared for greater triumphs awaiting her in the coming decade when she would play more mature, deeply emotional (and most generally emasculating) women.

The Gorgeous Hussy *(1936, M-G-M) with Robert Taylor*

Rain *(1932, United Artists) with Walter Huston*

Mannequin*(1938, M-G-M) with Spencer Tracy*

120

Dancing Lady *(1933, M-G-M) director Robert Z. Leonard, Oliver T. Marsh, Clark Gable and cameramen*

Our Blushing Brides *(1930, M-G-M) with Robert Montgomery*

Lost Horizon (1937)

It is unlikely that anyone will ever see *Lost Horizon* as originally filmed. Preview audiences so disliked the opening 20 minutes about a revolutionary upheaval in a fictitious Asian nation that director Frank Capra removed the footage and reportedly burned the negative. The final version began with the climax of that sequence and rapidly moved to its true subject, the idyllic land of Shangri-La, a paradise hidden in the Himalayas and presided over by a High Lama over 200 years old (played by 40-year-old Sam Jaffe) who is convinced that mankind is doomed to self-destruction. He has appointed himself custodian of man's greatest achievement—knowledge through books.

Adapted from James Hilton's novel, it had some of the same moralistic, simplistic clichés about honesty and learning from the past that marked Capra's other works (notably *Mr. Deeds Goes to Town*, 1936, and *Mr. Smith Goes to Washington*, 1939). There was something saccharine and simple-minded about Shangri-La, out of this world even by utopian standards, but the story (and no doubt the ideal) appealed to audiences in the 30s.

Appealing, too, was the film's huge scale. It was an extravagant production (reputedly costing over $2,000,000), with blizzards that looked like real snow (they were really crushed ice chips filmed in a Los Angeles cold-storage warehouse) and elaborate Art Deco sets. The picture earned a questionable nomination for best picture of the year, while well-deserved Oscars were awarded to art director Stephen Goosson and editors Gene Milford and Gene Havlick. Perhaps more significantly, in following Capra's earlier successes—*It Happened One Night*, 1934, and *Mr. Deeds Goes to Town*—it helped lift Columbia Pictures from poverty-row status into the front rank of Hollywood studios.

Margo and John Howard

Ronald Colman and Jane Wyatt

Margo and Ronald Colman

122

Ronald Colman and Sam Jaffe

Edward Everett Horton, Isabel Jewell, John Howard, Ronald Colman, Thomas Mitchell and servants

Dorothy Lamour as Marama, Jon Hall as Terangi and Kuulei De Clercq as Tita

Thomas Mitchell and Pauline Steele deliver Mamo Clark's baby during the height of the hurricane

The Hurricane (1937)

The spectacular hurricane of the film's title was in design, production and filming for four months. On screen it lashes the tropical island of Manekoora for twenty breathtaking minutes. James Basevi, who put this giant storm together, constructed a complete native village that included a fake lagoon, 600-foot beach frontage, docks, huts, church and palm trees. For the purpose of destruction he had airplane engines mounted across the lagoon and fire hoses ready to produce the torrential downpour. When the tidal wave hit, director John Ford himself pushed a series of buttons that released 2,000 gallons of water from chutes placed strategically around the village. To make the effect complete, Thomas Moulton contributed his Academy Award-winning sound recording.

Audiences, however, were blissfully unaware of the machinations behind the tempest and saw only the handsome Jon Hall struggling against the unleashed fury of nature to save his wife, the eternally saronged Dorothy Lamour, and the governor's wife, Mary Astor, from death. Audiences asked for nothing more than the lush island setting, the collossal conflict and the star-studded cast that included C. Aubrey Smith, Thomas Mitchell and Raymond Massey. It obviously didn't matter that the story was slight; filmgoers flocked to the theaters and made *The Hurricane* one of the top grossers of 1937.

Jon Hall silences prison warden John Carradine

Natives struggling against the hurricane in an attempt to reach the safety of the church

Ronald Colman (1891–1958)

After appearing on the British stage and screen, Colman emigrated to the U. S. in the early 20s and by 1925 was a top name in Hollywood. His big test came when Goldwyn cast him in his first talkie, *Bulldog Drummond*, 1929. Colman fans were delighted to find that he had a voice that matched his appearance, smooth and gentle, yet completely authoritative. Ronald Colman set a vocal standard for talking pictures as yet unmatched. When the 30s dawned Colman was one of the few silent stars who had successfully made the transition to talkies.

He appeared in 14 films during the 30s, most of which were big hits, thanks to the Colman combination of restraint, charm and talent, and many remain memorable. His first role of the 30s was the jewel thief in *Raffles*, 1930. Next he played the title character in John Ford's *Arrowsmith*, 1931, and then was the hero of *Cynara*, 1932. He was *Clive of India*, 1935 (in which he revealed himself for the first time *sans* mustache). Also in 1935 Colman gave one of his finest performances as Sidney Carton in the spectacular Dickens classic *A Tale of Two Cities*.

His last three films of the 30s were costumers. In 1937 he played the hero in James Hilton's *Lost Horizon* (see page 122), then he put the kingdom of Ruritania on moviedom's map with his dual role in *The Prisoner of Zenda*, 1937 (see page 127), and in 1938 portrayed François Villon in *If I Were King*.

Despite the fact that Colman was approaching 50, his career was still going strong. Perhaps it continued so long because there was never anyone quite like Ronald Colman in the history of motion pictures. He had just about everything—charm, dignity, serenity and just the right amount of aristocratic hauteur. He could be dashing, daring and yet be the tenderest of lovers. Men liked him even though their wives and girl friends swooned when he appeared on the screen. His glamour, class, talent and, of course, that marvelous voice would keep him in the star lineup throughout the 40s, win him an Oscar for *A Double Life*, 1948, and make him one of the most memorable of Hollywood figures.

The Devil to Pay *(1930, United Artists)*
with Loretta Young

Cynara *(1932, United Artists) with Kay Francis*

Members of the court in If I Were King *(1938, Paramount)*

Clive of India *(1935, United Artists, 20th Century) with Loretta Young*

The Prisoner of Zenda (1937)

This David O. Selznick production was based on Anthony Hope's novel, popular for 40 years, which was turned into a successful stage play and later was twice made into silent pictures (with James K. Hackett, 1913, and Ramon Novarro, 1922). It boasted an elegant, predominantly British cast, including Ronald Colman, Madeleine Carroll, Douglas Fairbanks, Jr., Raymond Massey, David Niven, Mary Astor and C. Aubrey Smith; a court setting that was one of the most pretentious interiors ever constructed for a movie; thrilling sword duels between Colman and Fairbanks, Jr.; enough villains, intrigue, action and romance for three movies; plus breath-taking sepia-toned photography that was rarely employed again because audiences preferred the newly perfected Technicolor process. Under John Cromwell's direction it was one of 1937's most entertaining movies.

The film is dominated by the suave, sophisticated presence of Mr. Colman in his second dual role (the first was in *Masquerader*, 1933) as an Englishman who agrees to double for the king of Ruritania during his coronation, his marriage and the foiling of plotters against the throne. Miss Carroll makes a lovely queen, and David Niven is impressive in a brief appearance. As the villains, Fairbanks, Jr.'s, roguish, agile playing is remarkably reminiscent of his father's screen image, and Raymond Massey creates a terrifying Black Duke Michael. For swashbuckling excitement, this was an on-land adventure every bit as thrilling as Errol Flynn's epics on the high seas.

Madeleine Carroll as the Ruritanian Princess Flavia

Douglas Fairbanks, Jr., as Rupert of Hentzau and Ronald Colman as Rudolph Rassendyl

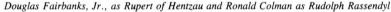

Madeleine Carroll and Ronald Colman as King Rudolf V

Joel McCrea with wife Frances Dee (1934)

Joel McCrea (1905–)

Throughout the 30s Joel McCrea epitomized Hollywood's "most amiable young man." He was always dependable, middle-of-the-road, all-American, athletic. He parlayed his clean-cut good looks, broad chest and shoulders and winning grin into 35 years of film success. As an actor, he seldom did anything more demanding than ride a horse, shoot a gun, save a damsel in distress or fill out a tuxedo handsomely. His voice was inexpressive, and he was master of three facial expressions: the smile, the frown and the stare.

However, McCrea's good looks and quiet style outweighed his deficits, and he became one of the decade's most sought-after leading men. McCrea began his career as an extra and only two years later, in 1929, began to get small parts in films like *The Jazz Age, The Single Standard* (which starred Garbo) and *So This Is College*. In the same year he also won a juvenile lead in *Dynamite*. He was now established. When the 30s dawned he was co-starring with Hollywood's important actresses. He played opposite Constance Bennett in four of his early films and later played opposite Miriam Hopkins in five films. He also co-starred with other stars like Merle Oberon, Dolores Del Rio, Barbara Stanwyck and Frances Dee (whom he married in 1933).

In all of the nearly 40 films he made in the 30s he was as relaxed and attractive in tuxedos in drawing-room dramas as he was in jeans and spurs in Westerns. He had no great pretensions about his acting ability nor any great magnetism on the screen. He simply did his work (many times in roles that, it was rumored, were Cooper rejects). On occasion his work was done exceptionally well, as in *These Three,* to which he lent several distinguished moments. McCrea's career peaked in the early 40s, and thereafter he specialized in Western roles until his retirement in 1962 after he made *Ride the High Country.*

Silver Horde (1930, RKO) with Louis Wolheim, Evelyn Brent and Raymond Hatton

Splendor (1935, United Artists) with Miriam Hopkins

128

Miriam Hopkins (1902–1972)

She was blonder than blond. Whenever she smiled her eyes crinkled delightfully at the corners. Her body was a designer's dream, and she used it gracefully and with style. It was no fluke that she became one of the top-ranking stars of the 30s.

After establishing a reputation as a fine stage actress, Miriam Hopkins made her screen debut in *Fast and Loose* in 1931. Her first screen success came the next year when she played Ivy, the barmaid for whom Fredric March's Dr. Jekyll lusted whenever he turned into Mr. Hyde. The roles that followed were starring roles, and her co-stars were among Hollywood's best—Gary Cooper, Joel McCrea, Edward G. Robinson and Paul Muni. She often played society ladies and romantic heroines but occasionally appeared as more hard-boiled types, such as the wanton devil-may-care girl in *The Story of Temple Drake*, 1933, the arch-conniver in the first all-Technicolor film, *Becky Sharp*, 1935, and a saloon keeper in *Barbary Coast*, 1935. Critics and fans alike acclaimed the latter as her best performance. "I enjoy playing that sort of woman," she once explained to an interviewer. "They have the courage of the damned. They know what they want and they go right ahead."

In the beginning of her career Hopkins held a contract with Paramount with a unique clause that allowed her to work on stage six months of the year. In 1934 the contract expired, and she was signed by Goldwyn, who loaned her to RKO and Korda. Despite this multistudio exposure, satisfactory scenarios continued to elude her, and by the time the 30s drew to a close her star had dimmed. Her last film of the decade was *The Old Maid*, 1939, in which her co-star, Bette Davis, got most of the footage. Although her stage career continued for many years thereafter, her appearances in films were infrequent after 1940.

Dr. Jekyll and Mr. Hyde *(1932, Paramount)*

Becky Sharp *(1935, RKO)*

Woman Chases Man *(1937, United Artists) with Joel McCrea*

The Story of Temple Drake *(1933, Paramount)*

129

Irene Dunne wreaking havoc on Cary Grant's curls

The Awful Truth (1937)

The Awful Truth joined Cary Grant and Irene Dunne in an irresistibly wacky comedy directed by Leo McCarey. The awful truth is that Lucy Warriner and her husband, Jerry, want a divorce, but everything about them suggests the only way they can be happy is to stay together. It is not much of a plot, and the lesson is fairly transparent, but its unraveling treats viewers to a gleeful ninety minutes until the stars understand it as well.

Being stubborn, the warring Warriners insist that a judge divorce them. The judge, a sagacious public official, gives them a ninety-day interlocutory decree, during which time it will become clear if they wish to be divorced. To convince herself it's over, Irene Dunne lets Ralph Bellamy, playing a young back-thumping, wide-mouth Oklahoman named Daniel Leeson, propose to her. She accepts so readily that Bellamy sweeps her up, whirls her about and whoops, "Wait until Ah tell Mama!" Not to be outdone, Grant's Jerry Warriner becomes engaged to a simpering aristocrat, Barbara Vance. In seeking revenge they achieve what borders on insanity—hilarious insanity. The film was such a big hit that it came to represent the craziness of the era.

It was based, like an earlier (1929) version, on a 1922 play by Arthur Richman, but Leo McCarey's direction (for which he won an Academy Award) differed from the stage production not only in style but in sensibility. Undeterred by Richman's thinly plotted play, McCarey skillfully wove giddy comedy in and out of the plot's basic assumption that the Warriners were always meant for each other. Freed by this self-evident truism, the story achieves its own frantic momentum. *The Awful Truth* delivered not only the how and why of the love battles of Lucy and Jerry Warriner but a sharply etched cavalcade of ridiculous aristocrats and hayseeds, all of whom are relentlessly dragged into the Warriner fight. On screen the supporting characters resist with all their might. In the audience, all howl with delight, knowing nobody will escape.

Irene Dunne and Cary Grant playing the zany Warriners

Irene Dunne, Alexander D'Arcy and Cary Grant

Irene Dunne as Lucy and Cary Grant as Jerry

130

Irene Dunne (1904–   )

Like so many of the 30s screen stars, pretty, ladylike Irene Dunne arrived in Hollywood via the stage. She made her film debut in a musical comedy, *Leathernecking*, 1930, and the next year played a dramatic role in *Cimarron*, for which she won an Academy Award nomination and star status. Her success in this film nearly sealed her fate, for although her next film was a comedy, *Bachelor Apartment*, 1931, the films that followed were, for the most part, successful melodramas, sometimes referred to as four-handkerchief films. She suffered ill-fated love affairs in *The Great Lover*, 1931, *Consolation Marriage*, 1931, *Symphony of Six Million*, 1932, and *Back Street*, 1932, and in 1933 and 1934 she appeared almost exclusively in dramas that had thwarted or divided love as their themes.

In 1935 she broke from her long-suffering, weepy image and appeared in two musicals. Warners signed her for *Sweet Adeline*, and then RKO starred her with Fred Astaire and Ginger Rogers in *Roberta*. Though these two films did well, they did not provide a complete turn-around for her career. She and audiences wept through *The Magnificent Obsession*, 1935, and a melodramatic version (with songs attached) of *Show Boat*, 1936. Dunne's leap to superstardom as a comedienne came when Columbia signed her to star opposite Melvyn Douglas in a small-town-girl-writes-bestseller story called *Theodora Goes Wild*. Of her performance, Graham Greene wrote: "Miss Irene Dunne will be remembered for many patient, womanly and rather smug performances . . . now she has been regroomed and appears as one of the best comediennes on the screen in the best light comedy since *Mr. Deeds*."

From Theodora, Dunne moved into the musical *High, Wide and Handsome*, 1937, and then in the same year to the riotously funny *The Awful Truth* (see page 130). The following year she made another musical, *The Joy of Living*, with Douglas Fairbanks, Jr., and in 1939 she was back to melodrama again. But by this time her reputation for light, wonderful, wacky comedy was as firmly established as the one she earned for moving, if sentimental, drama and melodrama.

Show Boat *(1936, Universal) with Allan Jones*

Back Street *(1932, Universal) with Charles Boyer*

Theodora Goes Wild *(1936, Columbia) with Melvyn Douglas*

Magnificent Obsession *(1935, Universal)*
with Robert Taylor

131

Marie Antoinette (1938)

Norma Shearer in the title role

Promoted as "The Life, the Sins of a Royal Bad-Girl!", this lavishly overproduced pageant returned Norma Shearer to the screen after her temporary retirement following the death of her husband, Irving Thalberg. Publicity copy declared that this "true story" of Marie Antoinette, the woman, was authentic in every detail, which surely meant only by Hollywood standards. In any event, no film since D. W. Griffith's _Intolerance_, 1916, had been so sumptuously costumed, complete with exaggerated wigs, oceans of feathers and fantastic gowns (including one for Shearer that resembled exploding fireworks), nor boasted more extravagantly decorated sets. Ultimately, the film was more a tribute to the creative imaginations of Adrian and Cedric Gibbons, the designers, than to the court of Louis XVI.

As the spirited, colorful Antoinette, Shearer was never more compelling and intelligent and for her performance received her sixth Oscar nomination. Tyrone Power provided attractive and persuasive support in a relatively limited role as her lover, Count Axel de Fersen. But the most spectacular performance in the film was Robert Morley's childishly cruel Louis XVI. In his film debut, slightly reminiscent of the young Charles Laughton, he was remarkably effective, making a character with few redeeming qualities somehow sympathetic. For his performance he was named as one of 1938's best actors by the National Board of Review. Gladys George also gave a superb performance in the brief role of Madame du Barry.

Although director W. S. Van Dyke did not, perhaps, give the film as much form and substance as he might have, and despite the fact that Thalberg's expert doctoring was missing, _Marie Antoinette_ made a nice showing among the other costume dramas of the 30s and proved to be very good entertainment.

Tyrone Power as Count Axel de Fersen

Tyrone Power receives a ring from his queen, Norma Shearer

Gladys George as Mme Du Barry

Joseph Schildkraut, Tyrone Power, Anita Louise, Norma Shearer and Reginald Gardiner

Robert Morley, Marilyn Knowlden, Anita Louise, Scotty Beckett and Norma Shearer

Tyrone Power and Annabella

Tyrone Power and Annabella

Tyrone Power as Ferdinand de Lesseps and Annabella as Toni Pellerin struggle against the force of the raging sandstorm

Suez (1938)

After the 1936 success of *San Francisco*'s earthquake virtually every Hollywood studio plunged into making "spectaculars." Between 1936 and 1940 few features were considered complete unless they had a disaster or a catastrophe to heighten their box-office appeal. *The Good Earth*, 1937, and *Jezebel*, 1938, were such powerful dramas that the spectacular effects—the swarm of locusts and the yellow-jack epidemic—augmented rather than constituted the dramatic tension. However, *In Old Chicago*, 1938, and *The Hurricane*, 1937, had little to recommend them other than the burning of a city and the sweeping away of an island by 90-mile-an-hour winds and a million gallons of water. *Suez* belongs to this second category, for although it had a potentially dramatic subject, the building of the great canal linking the Mediterranean Sea with the Red Sea, producer Darryl F. Zanuck saw it primarily as a vehicle for igniting a thunderous explosion and staging a sand storm, which he advised the publicity men to promote as a "Simoon!", meaning "the combined forces of a hurricane, an earthquake and a howling desert twister!"

As for the plot, *Suez* recounts the tribulations of architect Ferdinand de Lesseps (Tyrone Power) as he directs the digging of the canal. The pace is slow-moving and the style rather turgid. The film shows him coping with the treachery of Louis Napoleon (Leon Ames) and his henchmen, with the false love of the Countess Eugenie De Montijo (Loretta Young) and the amorous advances of a desert nymph, Toni Pellerin (Annabella), who virtually rapes him, though we are led to believe he somehow resists her passion and her charms. By the film's end it is painfully obvious that his true love is the ditch. After so much advance publicity, such an impressive budget and three appealing stars like Mr. Power, Miss Young and Annabella, one certainly deserved more than an explosion and a *Simoon*!

Loretta Young and Tyrone Power

Tyrone Power and Loretta Young

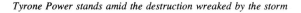

Tyrone Power stands amid the destruction wreaked by the storm

Annabella and Tyrone Power

135

Henry Hathaway (1898–   )

In the early 30s Paramount Studios signed former child-actor/assistant-director Henry Hathaway to a directing contract. He made his directorial debut with *Wild Horse Mesa*, 1932, the first of a series of "B" Westerns that would typify the bulk of his work during the coming years. His eleventh film, *Now and Forever*, 1934, however, elevated him to the front ranks of Paramount directors. He had a first-rate cast (Gary Cooper, Carole Lombard and Shirley Temple) and a somewhat sentimental story out of which Hathaway made a thoroughly entertaining film. His next film was the action-packed, big-budget adventure story *Lives of a Bengal Lancer*, 1935, with Gary Cooper. It was a resounding success, and Mr. Hathaway's direction received almost unanimous critical acclaim. Curiously, he chose for his next feature a gentle, romantic period drama, *Peter Ibbetson*, 1935. *Ibbetson* was not a box-office success, despite the haunting story, superb acting by Gary Cooper and Ann Harding and fine camera work by Lee Garmes.

Hathaway was one of the first directors to take the Technicolor cameras on location, as he did for *Trail of the Lonesome Pine*, 1936. That film was followed by the disastrous *Go West, Young Man*, 1936, starring Mae West at her absolute worst. He redeemed himself with *Souls at Sea*, 1937, another adventure story and one of the year's more popular movies. In it George Raft gave a remarkably affecting performance, and Hathaway used Raft as the star of his next film, *Spawn of the North*, 1938. *The Real Glory*, 1939, was Henry Hathaway's last film of the 30s, as well as his fourth with Gary Cooper. In 1940 he joined 20th Century–Fox and remained there almost exclusively until 1960.

The Real Glory *(1939, United Artists) with Rochelle Hudson and Gary Cooper*

Souls at Sea *(1937, Paramount) with George Raft and Gary Cooper*

Now and Forever *(1934, Paramount) with Hathaway directing Shirley Temple (on float) and Gary Cooper*

Howard Hawks (1896–   )

One of Hollywood's most distinguished and versatile directors, he joined Paramount in 1919 following a brief career as a racing pilot and a World War I stint as a fighter pilot. He rose from prop-man to editor in 1922, became a scriptwriter in 1924 and directed his first feature, *The Road to Glory,* in 1926.

During the 30s he directed only 14 films, but they ran the gamut from Westerns, war films, gangster movies and zany comedies to musicals and adventure films. The first three years of the decade yielded "action" films such as *The Criminal Code*, 1931, *The Crowd Roars*, 1932, *Tiger Shark*, 1932, and the classic film portrait of the underworld, *Scarface, Shame of the Nation*, 1932. His piloting experience and fascination with the stress of flying filtered into *The Dawn Patrol*, 1930, *Ceiling Zero*, 1936, and *Only Angels Have Wings*, 1939. He moved from action-packed drama to screwball comedy with gems like *Twentieth Century*, 1934, and *Bringing Up Baby*, 1938.

He wrote many of his early scripts and collaborated closely with some of the best scriptwriters in Hollywood—with Ben Hecht on *Scarface*, *Viva Villa!*, 1934, and *Twentieth Century*; with novelist William Faulkner on *Today We Live*, 1933; on a 1936 remake of *The Road to Glory* and in the 40s on the celebrated *The Big Sleep*. His films were highly successful commercial entertainment, but he often worked in serious overtones about crisis-ridden America and human brotherhood. Starting with *Bringing Up Baby* in 1938 he produced all his own pictures, and he continued making films with great success throughout the 40s and 50s.

Come and Get It *(1936, United Artists, Samuel Goldwyn) co-directed with William Wyler. Joel McCrea, Edward Arnold and Frances Farmer*

Only Angels Have Wings *(1939, Columbia) with Rita Hayworth, Cary Grant and Jean Arthur*

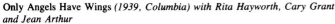

Today We Live *(1933, M-G-M) with Gary Cooper and Joan Crawford*

Henry Fonda and Bette Davis

Jezebel (1938)

Bette Davis's portrayal of the willful, neurotic Southern belle, Julie Marston, brought her superstardom and won for her a second Oscar. This time she earned it. It was not belated recognition for a past performance, as had been the case when she won for *Dangerous*, 1935, rather than for *Of Human Bondage*, 1934, for which she had not even been nominated. It was also a triumph of another sort: a vindication of her claim to Warner Brothers that she deserved better roles than the studio had given her prior to her defiant walkout and the court battles she had lost. More important, it proved she was an actress whose talents and volatile personality could totally dominate the screen. Her career was not that of the star-is-born variety but rather that of an artist hitting her stride, coming into her own.

There were those who criticized Miss Davis for capitalizing on the Julie Marston role as a none too subtle bid for the meatier, highly coveted part of Scarlett O'Hara in *Gone with the Wind*. The two parts did share a common ground—both dealt with headstrong, upper-crust, eyelash-batting Southern types. But if the charge were true, *Jezebel* was the most expensive screen test ever made! Davis never got to play Scarlett O'Hara, but in the role of Julie and in her famous scandalous red dress that showed its true colors even in the black-and-white film, she embodied the determined belle *par excellence*.

Fay Bainter's brilliant playing of her mother resulted in a unique and uneasy situation when Oscar night arrived. Both women found themselves nominated for best actress. Miss Bainter's nomination was for her lead role in *White Banners*, but she was also nominated in the supporting-actress category for *Jezebel*. Happily, both actresses were honored for their performances in *Jezebel*.

Bette Davis, in her infamous red dress, with Fay Bainter, Henry Fonda and Henry O'Neill

Bette Davis as Julie Marston

138

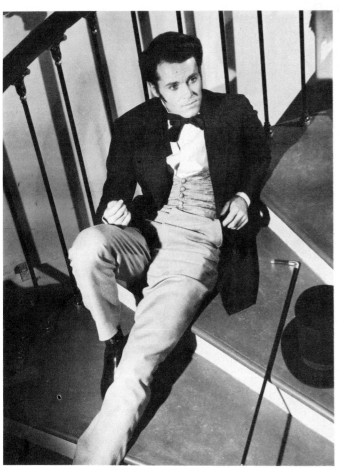

Henry Fonda as Pres Dillard

Bette Davis playing a willful Southern belle

Gordon Oliver, George Brent, Fay Bainter, Richard Cromwell, Henry O'Neill, Margaret Lindsay and Bette Davis

Mata Hari *(1931, M-G-M) with Ramon Novarro*

As You Desire Me *(1932, M-G-M) with Erich von Stroheim*

Anna Karenina *(1935, M-G-M) with Fredric March*

Conquest *(1937, M-G-M) with Charles Boyer*

140

Greta Garbo (1905–)

Her name evokes the mystery that made this elusive lady a legendary figure. From a job lathering men's faces in a Stockholm barbershop she became during the 30s the brightest star in the M-G-M firmament, first as an ingenue, then as a dramatic heroine and later, in an effort to buttress her sagging box-office appeal, as a bouncy comedienne. But the "new" Garbo failed to captivate the general public and outraged her spirited devotees, and in 1941 she retreated inside a cocoon from which she never emerged.

The beautiful Garbo entered the Swedish cinema in 1922 and first won recognition in Mauritz Stiller's *The Story of Gosta Berling*, 1924. Louis B. Mayer lured Stiller to Hollywood as an M-G-M director only by agreeing to sign his protégé to a three-year contract. Mayer thought Greta too fat, but after silents like *The Torrent*, 1926, the studio realized it had latched onto a hot property. By the time the 30s dawned she was a star whose capacity for voracious love-making left audiences breathless.

With the slogan "Garbo talks!" M-G-M released her first sound feature, *Anna Christie*, in 1930. Audiences waited with mounting excitement until, 34 minutes into the film, Garbo demanded "viskey with chincher ale." Her accent pleased viewers, and she followed with hugely successful *Susan Lenox: Her Fall and Rise*, 1931, *Mata Hari*, 1932, and *Grand Hotel*, 1932.

Queen Christina, 1933, brought rave reviews but only mixed box-office success. Her acting was top-notch in *Anna Karenina*, 1935, and in *Camille*, 1936, which is considered her best performance (and yielded her first Oscar nomination), but the public began to prefer Sonja Henie on ice to Garbo in another historical pageant. Comedy became the remedy and "Garbo laughs!" the slogan. The picture was *Ninotchka*, and audiences flocked to see Garbo as a no-nonsense Communist who succumbs to Western ways through the charms of Melvyn Douglas and Paris. Her final film, *Two-Faced Woman*, 1941, missed the mark, but Garbo's image lingers on, forever enigmatic, the eternal illusion.

Anna Christie *(1930, M-G-M)*

Susan Lennox—Her Fall and Rise*(1931, M-G-M) with Clark Gable*

Ninotchka *(1939, M-G-M) with Melvyn Douglas*

Queen Christina *(1933, M-G-M) with John Gilbert*

141

Tyrone Power highlighted by the flames that ravaged Chicago

Chicagoans fleeing the fire started by Mrs. O'Leary's cow

In Old Chicago (1938)

Hollywood seldom passes up a chance to take advantage of a good thing. The good thing in this case was the enthusiastic box-office reaction in the 30s to disasters and destruction. What could have more appeal, thought producers at 20th Century–Fox, than a fire that nearly demolishes an entire city? Thus, *In Old Chicago* was created.

To give the fire greater impact the studio constructed a realistic set that reflected the atmosphere of 1871 Chicago. To give the story romance it cast Alice Faye in the role of singer Belle Fawcett, gave her some sentimental numbers to sing, such as "I've Taken a Fancy to You" and "I'll Never Let You Cry," and cast opposite her Tyrone Power as Dion O'Leary. To insure box-office appeal it fleshed out the cast with such well-known names as Alice Brady, Don Ameche, Andy Devine, Brian Donlevy and Sidney Blackmer. And it dressed its actors in lavish period costumes.

The plot, based on a story by Niven Busch, included such elements as family relationships, personal heroism and corrupt politics, all set against the background of Chicago before and during the fire. These provided both an intimate view and an overview of the residents of the Windy City. Essential to the plot, of course, was Mrs. O'Leary's cow that kicks over a lamp and ignites the city.

Audiences flocked to see *In Old Chicago* and made it a financial success. Successful, too, was Alice Brady's rendering of Molly O'Leary, the owner of the clumsy bovine. Her portrayal won her an Oscar for best supporting actress.

Tyrone Power, Alice Faye and Don Ameche

Alice Brady and Tyrone Power

Tyrone Power as Dion O'Leary and Alice Faye as Belle Fawcett

Don Ameche and Tyrone Power

Claire Trevor as Jo Keller and Humphrey Bogart as Rocks Valentine

The Amazing Dr. Clitterhouse (1938)

Edward G. Robinson's Dr. Clitterhouse earns the description "amazing" by committing the perfect crime. Using a loophole in legal logic, Clitterhouse convinces a jury that he is technically innocent of Rocks Valentine's murder by, first, copping a plea of insanity and then testifying that he was sane when he poisoned Rocks (Humphrey Bogart). The jury decides that his testimony is indeed one of a mentally unstable man and acquits him.

As the research scientist who joins a group of thieves to collect firsthand data for his study of the criminal mind, Robinson effectively broke his snarling "Little Caesar" image, if only temporarily. Though, as the gang's leader, he seems to enjoy guiding the thieves into more daring and profitable jobs and researching and committing his perfect crime, he is able to maintain a strange appeal and, in the eyes of the audience, remains a crook only in the interest of science.

Claire Trevor's role of Jo Keller, the jewel thieves' fence, adds glamour and sophistication to the bad-girl screen image she created with her pathetic streetwalker in *Dead End*, 1937. In that film she also played opposite Bogart, but in a minor role. In *Clitterhouse*, she has a role equal in size to Bogart's and proves herself to be every bit as compelling as he. One knows during the course of their romance, from their tender embraces to their knock-down fights, that the petty, hot-tempered Rocks doesn't stand a chance against the cool, tough but feminine Jo.

Edward G. Robinson as the title character and Claire Trevor

Humphrey Bogart, Edward G. Robinson and Maxie Rosenbloom on the job

Claire Trevor and Humphrey Bogart, members of the jewel-theft ring

144

William A. Wellman (1896–   )

With his reputation as a director primarily based on Paramount Studio's *Wings*, 1927 (which won the first best-picture Oscar and gave Gary Cooper his first important role), Mr. Wellman began the 30s under exclusive contract to Warner Brothers. Between 1930 and 1933 he directed 16 features, only three of which were better than average programmers: *The Public Enemy*, 1931, *The Hatchet Man*, 1932, and *Wild Boys of the Road*, 1933. The remainder, although entertaining, were more impressive for their volume than for any unique or inspired directorial touches. Collectively, they might be regarded as characteristic of his 33-year career. His work is so uneven, his directorial point of view so illusive, his forte so difficult to isolate that he is best characterized as Hollywood's middle-of-the-road craftsman.

Arriving in Hollywood in 1921, Wellman, a former pilot and Foreign Legionnaire, worked as an actor until he got his first directorial assignment on *The Man Who Won*, 1923. Except for *Wings,* none of his other silent pictures was particularly memorable. After his Warner contract expired in 1933 he worked as an independent on *Stingaree*, 1934, for RKO-Radio Pictures; *Call of the Wild*, 1935, for Darryl F. Zanuck's new Twentieth-Century Pictures; and then signed with David O. Selznick for two Technicolor productions, *A Star Is Born* and *Nothing Sacred*, in 1937. These two represent the very finest of Mr. Wellman's 30s films. He and collaborator Robert Carson won an Oscar for best story for *A Star Is Born*, and with a delightful Ben Hecht script he turned *Nothing Sacred* into classic screwball comedy fare. In the next two years he directed three features, only one of which was outstanding, *Beau Geste*, 1939. Throughout the 40s and 50s he was seldom idle, and if none of his films was great, at least one, *The Ox-Bow Incident*, 1943, created considerable controversy with its provocative lynching story. He returned to his great love for the airplane with the popular *The High and the Mighty*, 1954, and subsequently made action films. The last of his features, to date, is *Lafayette Escardrille*, 1958.

The Hatchet Man *(1932, Warner Brothers) with Loretta Young and Edward G. Robinson*

Stingaree *(1934, RKO) with Irene Dunne and Richard Dix*

A Star Is Born *(1937, United Artists, Selznick International) with Janet Gaynor and Fredric March*

Nothing Sacred *(1937, United Artists, Selznick International) with Fredric March, Carole Lombard and Walter Connolly*

Two youngsters from the Midwest, a cartoonist named Walt Disney and his business-oriented borther Roy, made a short animated film called Steamboat Willie *in the 20s, the hero of which eventually turned into Mickey Mouse. In 1937 Walt stunned and delighted the entire world with a full-length animated cartoon in color,* Snow White and the Seven Dwarfs. *It turned out to be the first of many Disney delights, and although the Disney techniques of animation grew progressively more sophisticated, none ever exceeded the charm of Dopey, Sneezy, Grumpy, Sleepy, Happy, Bashful and Doc. The songs were top-notch, the humor was delightful, and a century hence it will still remain a great, great film.*

Young Mickey Rooney and canine pal in The Adventures of Huckleberry Finn *(1939)*

The Marx Brothers— Chico (1891–1961),

Harpo (1894–1964), Groucho (1895–   ), Zeppo (1901–   )

Groucho (Julius Henry Marx)

Their father was a tailor known as "Misfit Marx." Their mother, Minnie, was the sister of Al Shean, who with his partner almost turned their "Oh, Mr. Gallagher, Yes, Mr. Shean" song into a national anthem. Minnie's heart was set on seeing all five of her boys onstage and successful. One brother, Gummo, escaped, while Zeppo, after playing juvenile leads and singing infrequently in early Marx Brothers epics, later fled the act.

The brothers began on the vaudeville circuit and in the 20s convulsed Broadway audiences in *The Cocoanuts* and *Animal Crackers*, which were later converted (in 1929 and 1930) into their first and second pictures. Nobly aided and abetted by scripts written by such brilliant humorists as George S. Kaufman and S. J. Perelman, they made light, howlingly funny movies during the 30s. They always played the same basic roles. Groucho, with mustache and cigar, was invariably the phony tycoon, with the stride of a demented pelican and a custom of making passionate overtures (usually to Margaret Dumont) one minute and turning violently abusive the next. Harpo, blond-wigged and wide-eyed, was the pantomimist supreme, with a habit of chasing any female that came within range and, halfway through the film, playing the harp rather well. Chico always dressed like an Italian organ grinder, talked with an accent that was part Neapolitan, part delicatessen and inevitably played a one- or two-fingered piano sonata.

Why, then, as they made *Monkey Business*, 1931, *Duck Soup*, 1933, *A Night at the Opera*, 1935, *A Day at the Races*,1937, and a number of others, didn't audiences tire of them? They didn't have the pathos and deep humanity of a Chaplin or a Keaton, nor were they put upon like W. C. Fields. It is hard to describe their appeal. Clearly, they were products of the twentieth century—caustic, basically cynical, with a streamlined lunacy all their own.

Harpo (Adolph Arthur Marx)

Chico (Leonard Marx)

Room Service *(1938, RKO) with Harpo, Chico, Lucille Ball and Groucho*

148

At the Circus *(1939, M-G-M) with Groucho and Margaret Dumont*

A Night at the Opera *(1935, M-G-M) with Groucho, Chico, Allan Jones, Harpo and ship stewardesses*

A few of the more effective movie ads of the 30s

150

A GREAT CLASSIC COMES TO LIFE
IN GLORIOUS TECHNICOLOR!

SHIRLEY TEMPLE
in THE
LITTLE PRINCESS

Shirley!...at last in
TECHNICOLOR

with
RICHARD GREENE
ANITA LOUISE
IAN HUNTER · CESAR ROMERO
ARTHUR TREACHER · MARY NASH
SYBIL JASON · MILES MANDER
MARCIA MAE JONES

A 20th Century-Fox Picture
Darryl F. Zanuck in Charge of Production

ANOTHER GRAND PICTURE OPENS THE GATES OF MEMORY...
rich with the emotion of years of beloved melody!

Darryl F. Zanuck and 20th
Century-Fox bring you the new-
est and greatest in entertainment!

The stars of "Alexander's Ragtime Band"
TYRONE POWER
ALICE FAYE
and the star who sings back
the past you want to remember
AL JOLSON
in
ROSE-OF
WASHINGTON
SQUARE

with
WILLIAM   JOYCE   HOBART
FRAWLEY · COMPTON · CAVANAUGH

A 20th Century-Fox Picture
DARRYL F. ZANUCK In Charge of Production
Directed by Gregory Ratoff

Four more good ads, but only The Wizard of Oz *hit the jackpot*

Follow THE YELLOW BRICK ROAD TO Oz

M-G-M'S GREATEST
ACHIEVEMENT!

Metro-Goldwyn-Mayer's Glorious Technicolor Triumph

THE WIZARD of OZ

with JUDY GARLAND (as Dorothy), FRANK MORGAN (as the Wizard), RAY BOLGER (as the Scare-crow), BERT LAHR (as the Cowardly Lion), JACK HALEY (as the Tin Woodman), BILLIE BURKE (as the Good Witch), MARGARET HAMILTON (as the Bad Witch), CHARLEY GRAPEWIN (as Uncle Henry) and the Munchkins · Screenplay by Noel Langley, Florence Ryerson and Edgar Allan Woolf · A VICTOR FLEMING Production · Produced by MERVYN LE ROY · Directed by VICTOR FLEMING

Nobodies on the road to Nowhere!

WARNER BROS. OFFER
JOHN GARFIELD
and PRISCILLA LANE
in "DUST BE MY DESTINY"

with ALAN HALE · Frank McHugh · Billy Halop · Directed by LEWIS SEILER · Screen Play by Robert Rossen · From a Novel by Jerome Odlum · A First National Picture

You Can't Take It with You (1938)

The title suggests that we might as well live for today and enjoy doing exactly what we like, and this is precisely what each member of the Sycamore household does. Never have more delightfully bizarre and screwy characters been assembled on the screen, and under the expert direction of Frank Capra all their wacky indulgences are deliciously served up with old-fashioned humanness and just a touch of pathos, making this a picture worthy of its best-picture and best-director Oscars. It added new dimensions of poignancy and fun to the already superbly crafted Kaufman-and-Hart stage play.

Jean Arthur is Alice, Grandpa Vanderhof's (Lionel Barrymore's) favorite granddaughter and the only responsible member of the family. Spring Byington flutters about as the mother who fancies herself a playwright simply because someone left a typewriter in the house by mistake. The father who never outgrew adolescence and spends his time in the cellar making fireworks is played by Samuel Hinds, while Ann Miller, as Alice's sister, leaps and pirouettes about to the coachings of Mischa Auer, a rowdy Russian ballet master who imagines her a grand ballerina. Add to these an assortment of oddballs Grandpa has collected—an iceman who becomes a perpetual guest, a bookkeeper who makes toys, a married couple who constantly talk about xylophones while they cook—and this is one household in which things are never dull!

Into this pandemonium enters the shockingly sane son of a Wall Street millionaire with whom Alice has fallen in love. The contrast between the propriety of the Kirby family and the bedlam of Alice's clan set the stage for abundant laughs. James Stewart plays the young suitor, and Grandpa takes it upon himself to convince Stewart's millionaire father (Edward Arnold) that his is a shameful existence. At the end the staid gent is converted to the Sycamore–Vanderhof philosophy of gaiety, but only after many hysterically funny and often touching digressions. All ends well, with Stewart and Arthur married and the household back to its frantic, dizzying normalcy.

James Stewart, Jean Arthur, Dub Taylor, Lionel Barrymore, Spring Byington, Edward Arnold, Ann Miller, Mary Forbes, Mischa Auer, Lillian Yarbo, Eddie Anderson and Donald Meek

Frank Capra, director

Jean Arthur as Alice Sycamore

James Stewart as Tony Kirby

Frank Borzage (1893–1962)

Known for lyrical romances, Frank Borzage had 36 films to his credit when he won an Oscar for his poignant drama *Seventh Heaven*, 1927, about young Parisian lovers during World War I. His first part-talkie, *The River*, 1929, had a title card that beautifully encapsulated Borzage's attitude toward love and life. It read, "A river is like love, it cleanses all things." There was a glimpse of another dimension in Margaret Sullavan's line from *Little Man What Now?*, 1934: "We create life—why be afraid of it?"

Throughout the 30s his films had at their core a strong and gently compassionate view of mankind as well as a total abhorrence of war. His voice was particularly meaningful to Depression audiences in such films as *A Man's Castle*, 1933, the story of a young couple, Spencer Tracy and Loretta Young, suffering under the yoke of poverty. In *Young America*, 1931, and *Bad Girl*, 1931, for which he received a second Oscar, he focused on average people desperately struggling against their environment. One of his more artistic but commercially disappointing films was a disturbing antiwar allegory, *No Greater Glory*, 1934, about a neighborhood gang forced to defend their playground against a rival gang's take-over. The screen version of Hemingway's *A Farewell to Arms*, 1932, one of Borzage's best-known films, provided an ideal vehicle for his philosophical and artistic sensibilities, with its passionate though tragic love story and antiwar theme. The 30s were the high point of his art, and the films he directed periodically until shortly before his death failed to recapture his earlier flair.

A Man's Castle *(1933, Columbia) with Spencer Tracy and Loretta Young*

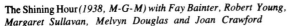

The Shining Hour *(1938, M-G-M) with Fay Bainter, Robert Young, Margaret Sullavan, Melvyn Douglas and Joan Crawford*

A Farewell to Arms *(1932, Paramount), Frank Borzage (center) directing Gary Cooper and Adolphe Menjou*

Lana Turner, perhaps a wee bit on the plump side, early in her career

Norma Shearer surveying her domain during the bell-bottomed 30s

James Stewart and Jean Arthur

Mr. Smith Goes to Washington (1939)

The last of Frank Capra's fine and funny films of the 30s took as its target nothing less than the Senate of the United States. James Stewart is the small-town boy who comes to Washington as a short-term Senator. As Jefferson Smith, he is kin to Longfellow Deeds (Gary Cooper) in Mr. Capra's early (1936) *Mr. Deeds Goes to Town*—wide-eyed, naïve, dedicated to democratic ideals. The story line is simple: When Mr. Smith discovers that his idol, Senator Joseph Paine (Claude Raines), is a crook and a grafter, he sets out to fight him and is adeptly framed by the crooked political machine. Luckily, he has the same experienced sidekick who helped Mr. Deeds in his time of trouble—his secretary, played by the delightful Jean Arthur. She helps him escape expulsion through a filibuster that lasts long enough for public opinion to be roused on a grand scale and comes to his aid. In the end democracy and the young Senator triumph, and the evil Senator repents.

For its time, this primitive Watergate tale was highly controversial. After a much publicized premiere in Washington's Constitution Hall, Senator Alben Barkley assailed *Mr. Smith* as a "grotesque distortion" of the truth. Ambassador to Great Britain Joseph Kennedy said it damaged America's reputation abroad and played into the hands of Adolf Hitler's propaganda machine. There were even reports that major Hollywood studios, fearing industry-wide censorship, offered to pay back all costs to Columbia Pictures to have it withdrawn.

On the other hand, millions agreed with Frank Nugent's *New York Times* review that it was "more fun even than the Senate itself." And to the audiences that loved it, James Stewart's impassioned rhetoric seemed to impart a new optimism about their country and the basically decent principles for which it stood. No one dreamed that more than three decades later an anonymous and lowly "Mr. Smith" would find a taped door in a rambling edifice called Watergate—and so begin to unravel a scandal that made Mr. Smith's discovery look tame.

James Stewart in the title role

James Stewart during his filibuster

Jack Carson, Paul Stanton, Thomas Mitchell and Jean Arthur

Golden Boy (1939)

Adapted from the stage hit by Clifford Odets, *Golden Boy* introduced a bright new face and talent to the screen, William Holden, as Joe, a promising young violinist who also boxed like an avenging angel. The film focuses dramatically on the young man's burning ambition and desire to help his working-class family by turning his "golden" hands into hard cash, not with the violin but in the boxing ring.

Director Rouben Mamoulian brought Lee J. Cobb to recreate his stage role as the father with high hopes for his son's artistic future. But Joe decides that boxing would bring more money faster. His clever manager and trainer (Adolphe Menjou) launches him on a championship career, while his sweetheart Lorna (Barbara Stanwyck) tries, without success, to convince him he doesn't belong in the fight racket and is merely a pawn for others.

The film climaxes with the Golden Boy's most important match. Victory will bring him within one step of the championship crown. He boxes with a ferocious, relentless determination to win, but his subsequent victory leaves his opponent dead. Joe agonizes over the terrible price he has paid for his fame, but at this point Mamoulian turns the plot into pure Hollywood pap. Instead of taking his life and Lorna's, as in the stage play, the film's final scene shows Miss Stanwyck consoling her man, assuring him that he will one day again play the violin.

William Holden wins the bout

William Holden, Don Beddoe, Adolphe Menjou and Barbara Stanwyck

Barbara Stanwyck as Lorna and William Holden as Joe Bonaparte

Rhett and Scarlett in one of the less tempestuous moments of their love affair

Vivien Leigh, as Scarlett O'Hara, among a sea of wounded Confederate soldiers in Atlanta

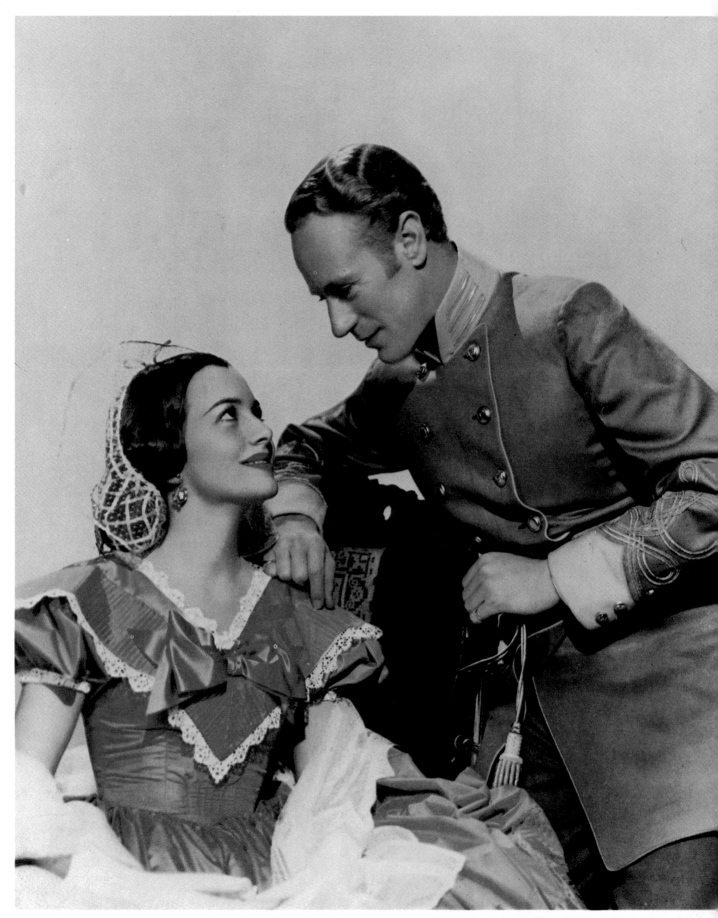

Olivia de Havilland, as Melanie, and Leslie Howard, as Ashley Wilkes, the two supporting actors who helped make Gone with the Wind *an all-time blockbuster*

Gone with the Wind (1939)

What can you say about a more than 35-year-old film that is still shown in first-run movie houses? Winner of eight Academy Awards, *Gone with the Wind* is certainly the greatest of the 30s productions, one of the all-time box-office bonanzas and a timeless film classic.

When producer David O. Selznick closed a deal for the film rights to Margaret Mitchell's phenomenal best seller he also began the greatest casting sweepstakes in the history of motion pictures. Almost every actor and actress in Hollywood coveted the lead roles, and many were screen-tested. Though Clark Gable (supposedly Mitchell's choice) was always in the front-running for the role of Rhett Butler, others were mentioned or discussed, including Gary Cooper, Ronald Colman and Fredric March. The list of actresses queuing up for the role of Scarlett O'Hara was astounding, among them Katharine Hepburn, Bette Davis, Norma Shearer, Jean Arthur, Tallulah Bankhead, Joan Bennett and Loretta Young. The film was well under way when the virtually unknown Vivien Leigh tested for and won the part.

Even after the cast was assembled, with Olivia de Havilland as Melanie, Leslie Howard as Ashley and Thomas Mitchell as Gerald O'Hara, things did not go smoothly. It original director, George Cukor, was let go after three weeks of shooting (supposedly on Gable's demand) and was replaced by Victor Fleming, who collapsed on the set shortly before the film's completion and left the finishing work to be done by Sam Wood. The original Sidney Howard screenplay was revised by writers such as F. Scott Fitzgerald, John Van Druten and Ben Hecht. Then Hecht, Selznick and Fleming reworked the rework before producing what became the final shooting script by returning to Sidney Howard's original conception.

Despite its production woes, *Gone with the Wind* is a beautiful film both visually and artistically. The atmosphere of the genteel South, of the devasting War between the States and of the back-breaking Reconstruction is recreated faithfully; and the actors, from the leads to the secondary players, capture the warmth, humanity and intricacies of their characters.

Vivien Leigh as Scarlett O'Hara

Clark Gable as Rhett Butler

Olivia de Havilland as Melanie Hamilton

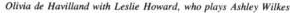

Olivia de Havilland with Leslie Howard, who plays Ashley Wilkes

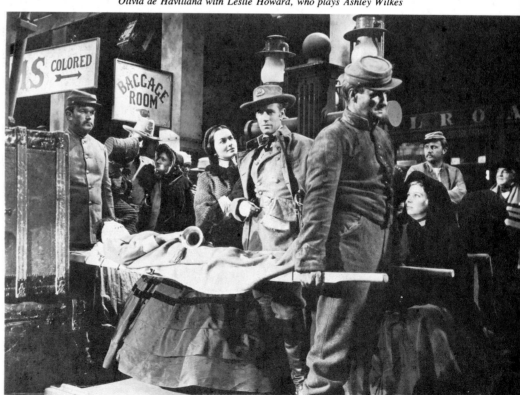

Vivien Leigh about to shoot Yankee deserter Paul Hurst

Clark Gable and Vivien Leigh outside Aunt Pittypat's house in Atlanta

Vivien Leigh and Thomas Mitchell, as Gerald O'Hara, work to restore Tara

161

Vivien Leigh in search of Dr. Meade during the evacuation of Atlanta

Wicked Witch of the West Margaret Hamilton spying on Judy Garland and Ray Bolger

Ray Bolger as the Scarecrow, Judy Garland as Dorothy, Bert Lahr as the Cowardly Lion and Jack Haley as the Tin Woodman

The Wizard of Oz (1939)

The Wizard of Oz opens with a dedication to the "young at heart." It is possibly the most delightful present Hollywood ever created for young or old. Judy Garland played Dorothy (only after M-G-M couldn't get Shirley Temple), the wide-eyed young girl from Kansas who dreams that she is swept away from home by a tornado with only her dog Toto for company. The storm deposits her in the magical Technicolor land of Oz, and before she wakes up and returns to the loving hearth of her adoring Uncle Henry and Aunty Em, she follows the legendary yellow-brick road in search of the Wizard himself (played by an infectious humbug, Frank Morgan).

On her enchanting journey she encounters three marvelous personifications of human frailty—the Cowardly Lion (Bert Lahr), the Scarecrow with no brain (Ray Bolger) and the defenseless Tin Woodman (Jack Haley). Like Dorothy, they prove triumphant but only after standing up to Margaret Hamilton's cackling Wicked Witch of the West. Aided by winged lower primates with the deadliest expression imaginable, the Wicked Witch is determined to stop Dorothy and her friends. But she is foiled by the Good Witch of the East (Billie Burke).

Dorothy and company succeed because they abide by the prescription of L. Frank Baum's original story: believe, and the rest will follow. Nothing evokes Baum's theme more than the song Dorothy sings while still in her native Kansas. Dreaming of something lovelier than the endless expanse of Midwestern plains, she looks up and sings, "Somewhere, over the rainbow . . . " It was an irresistible magnet for sentimentalists and romantics willing to believe and one that thrust Garland into superstardom and helped make this movie the most enduring of childhood-fantasy films.

Judy Garland replacing some of Ray Bolger's stuffing

Judy Garland given a beauty treatment by women of Emerald City

Jack Haley and Bert Lahr climbing toward the Wicked Witch's castle

163

Rouben Mamoulian (1898–)

Following an illustrious tenure directing on the Broadway stage, Russian-born Rouben Mamoulian made an impressive Hollywood debut with his early sound production *Applause*, 1929. He was 31 and had no previous film training, but he quickly became one of the industry's most capable directors.

He extended his reputation with innovative direction of his second film, *City Streets*, 1931, a gripping underworld drama that cast newcomer Sylvia Sydney alongside Gary Cooper. His *Dr. Jekyll and Mr. Hyde*, 1931, is still the best version of this perennially popular horror classic (Fredric March won an Oscar for his performance as the infamous split personality). It was a long way to *Queen Christina*, 1933, a lavish historical romance starring Greta Garbo in the title role, but the director proved himself equally at home. With *Becky Sharp*, 1935, he became the first to direct a full-length film entirely in color.

His stage-directing background led to several musicals, among them *Love Me Tonight*, 1932 (with Jeanette MacDonald and Maurice Chevalier), which he approached in a Lubitsch fashion, and *High, Wide and Handsome*, 1937. In 1935 he returned briefly to the Broadway theater as director of George Gershwin's *Porgy and Bess*.

One of his most famous touches was the last shot of Garbo at the helm of the ship in *Queen Christina*, an enormous close-up of an unforgettably enigmatic Garbo face that Mamoulian claims he obtained by telling her to "think of absolutely nothing." Unfortunately, several of his efforts in the late 30s—such as *The Gay Desperado*, 1936, and *We Live Again*, 1934—were little more than diverting matinee fare and hardly up to his earlier standards.

The Gay Desperado *(1936, Paramount) with Nino Martini and Ida Lupino*

We Live Again *(1934, United Artists, Samuel Goldwyn) Fredric March and Anna Sten*

City Streets *(1931, Paramount) with Gary Cooper and Rouben Mamoulian*

James Stewart (1908–   )

Tall, thin and wistful, young Jimmy Stewart graduated from Princeton and joined Joshua Logan's University Players. After some small roles on Broadway, he got his brilliant screen career off to an inauspicious start when he played a reporter in *Murder Man*, 1935, starring Spencer Tracy. The next year he appeared in eight films, including the one that gave him his first real break, *Born to Dance*, playing opposite Eleanor Powell. In the film he played a sailor and, believe it or not, introduced Cole Porter's enduring love song "Easy to Love." The following year he had co-star billing twice—opposite Simone Simon in *Seventh Heaven* and with Edward G. Robinson in *The Last Gangster*—and in 1938 he landed co-starring roles in *Of Human Hearts* with Beulah Bondi; *Vivacious Lady*, opposite Ginger Rogers; *Shopworn Angel*, reteamed with Margaret Sullavan; and *You Can't Take It with You*, ideally complemented by co-star Jean Arthur under Frank Capra's direction.

By 1939 Stewart was one of the most respected young actors in movies. David O. Selznick signed him for *Made for Each Other*, an unfortunately mundane script that he and Carole Lombard invested with a glow it never deserved. M-G-M called him back to star with Joan Crawford in *Ice Follies of 1939*, a preposterously inept attempt to cash in on the Sonja Henie ice-skating box-office bonanza. Fortunately, this fiasco was soon forgotten in the light of another comedy role in *It's a Wonderful World* opposite Claudette Colbert. Then Frank Capra asked for him again to play the title role in *Mr. Smith Goes to Washington*. It was a smash hit (see page 156). Stewart's last film of the 30s was another loan-out role opposite Marlene Dietrich in *Destry Rides Again*. He gave a strong, relaxed performance that possessed all the slightly nervous, arched-eyebrow, mumbling mannerisms that were to typify the Stewart screen personality in future years.

Rose Marie *(1936, M-G-M) with Jeanette MacDonald*

Seventh Heaven *(1937, 20th Century–Fox) with Simone Simon*

Small Town Girl *(1936, M-G-M) with Janet Gaynor and Robert Taylor*

Shopworn Angel *(1938, M-G-M) with Margaret Sullavan*

Tyrone Power as Major Rama Safti, Myrna Loy as Lady Edwina Esketh and George Brent as Tom Ransome

The Rains Came (1939)

When the rains came in 1939, it marked the final storm in a decade of screen extravaganzas. Producer Darryl F. Zanuck brought Louis Bromfield's best-selling novel to the screen in grand style, complete with all the romance, intrigue, suffering and action of the book. The production was in black and white, but no expense was spared the special-effects technicians, who engineered an earthquake, a breaking dam and flood and a falling temple.

Zanuck also assembled a first-rate cast headed by his top male contract star at 20th Century–Fox, Tyrone Power, in the lead role of a high-caste Indian surgeon, Major Safti. Myrna Loy was borrowed from M-G-M to play the spoiled Lady Esketh, a role outside Loy's customary "perfect wife" image, and George Brent was brought from Warner Brothers to play Tom Ransome, the indolent son of an earl who fritters his life away in the colonies. The film also introduced Zanuck's latest discovery, starlet Brenda Joyce, as a missionary's daughter who falls in love with Ransome. Maria Ouspenskaya led a strong supporting cast with a powerful performance as the wise Maharani.

The plot developed rather ingeniously, with the monsoons altering the lives of everyone in the Indian city of Ranchipur. Against this background of natural havoc Power tries desperately to resist a human catastrophe—the advances of Miss Loy, a lady who has already been married and must by the rules of his social caste be considered out of bounds. While the disasters mount, resistance is made more difficult by their being thrown together in treating the injured and dying. By the end, she has helped him through the floods and a cholera epidemic. The resolution, although a bit too pat, does get everyone off the hook: She contracts cholera and dies.

George Brent, Myrna Loy and Marjorie Rambeau

Myrna Loy and Tyrone Power as an earthquake shakes the city

166

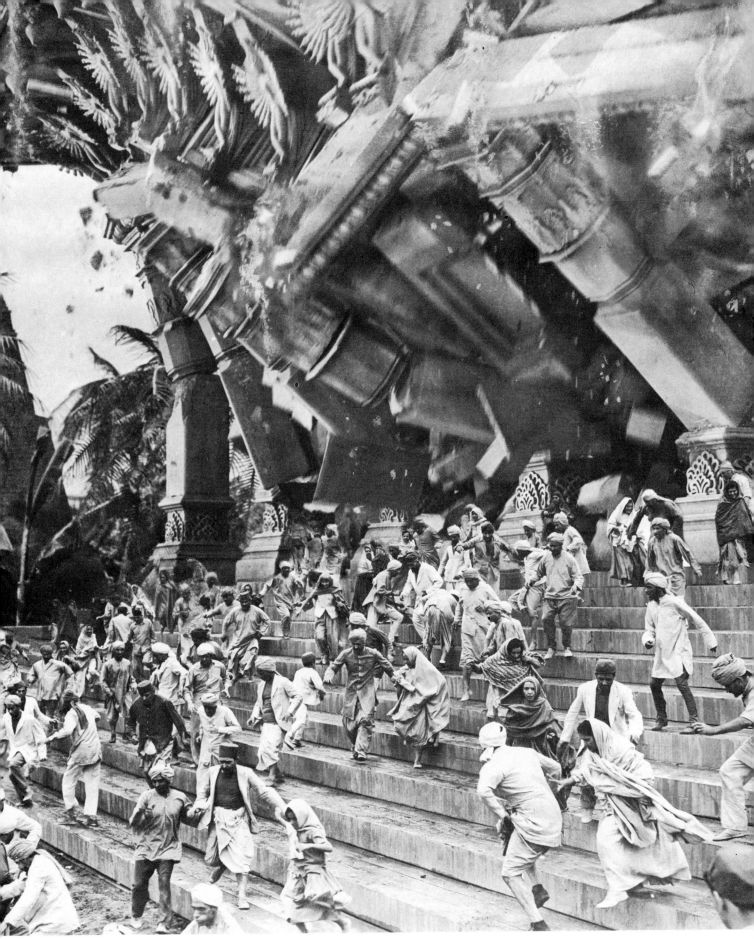

The collapse of the temple

Ida Lupino as Ann Brandon

The Adventures of Sherlock Holmes (1939)

It was the second film about the famous detective made in 1939 and it had the same stars as the first, *The Hound of the Baskervilles*, Basil Rathbone and Nigel Bruce. The fact that many one- and two-reel Sherlock Holmes adventures had already been made in several countries also had no effect on the movie's success. From the moment the public heard Rathbone turn to his closest friend, the doggedly amiable Dr. Watson (Bruce), and calmly say, "Elementary, my dear Watson," moviegoers knew they had found the quintessential Holmes.

Rathbone's enduring success as the eccentric sleuth (he played the role in 16 films) was the kind of casting miracle Hollywood dreams about. But *The Adventures of Sherlock Holmes* was one of the rare times he played the Baker Street hero in Arthur Conan Doyle's original setting (future versions showed him all over the modern world). Audiences were plunged directly into the heart of old London, the city Graham Greene described as composed of "cobbles, mud, fast cabs and gas-lamps." Character and atmosphere were captured with authenticity.

The story line was just as authentically Holmesian. Archenemy Professor Moriarty intends nothing less than the theft of the Crown Jewels from the Tower of London. Warned by Ida Lupino, who appears at the door to Holmes's digs as a frightened caller, the crack detective throws himself into the fray. Dr. Watson faithfully trails at his heels, while Mrs. Hudson (Mary Gordon) presides over the Holmes roost as the superbly dependable housekeeper.

Under Alfred Werker's direction, *The Adventures of Sherlock Holmes* transferred to the screen the heroic intrigue elaborated in Conan Doyle's stories. Villainy is afoot in the foggy capital. Only Sherlock Holmes can solve the mystery. Thank heavens there is Basil Rathbone to save the day with calm expertise and, above all, deadly accurate deduction. Thank heavens, too, that unlike his successors in the 40s director Werker had the sense to preserve Holmes in his London habitat rather than drop him in a modern metropolis.

Basil Rathbone as Sherlock Holmes

Guards and Scotland Yard inspectors check crown jewels

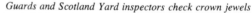

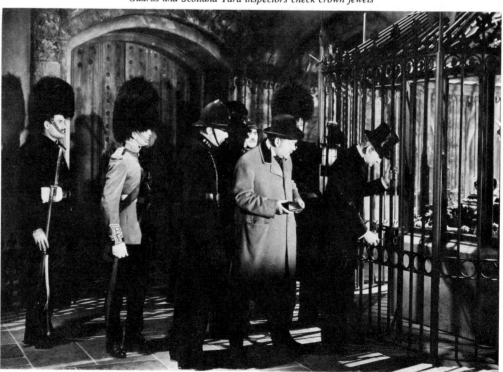

Basil Rathbone and Nigel Bruce, who plays Dr. Watson

Robert Donat (1905-1958)

Although he made but one film in the United States and relatively few in Great Britain, Donat will always be ranked among the most gracious, most appealing and most competent screen actors of the 30s. His life was a tragic one, plagued by recurring bouts with asthma and self-doubts which gravely inhibited his ability to make key career decisions.

He was discovered on the English stage by Alexander Korda. A supporting role in *The Private Life of Henry VIII,* 1932, made him an international name and encouraged Hollywood to lure him—on loan from Korda—for *The Count of Monte Cristo,* 1934, his first important film. Back in England the following year, he played Richard Hannay in Hitchcock's production of the spy yarn *The 39 Steps.* Along with Madeleine Carroll, Donat kept audiences perched breathlessly on the edge of their seats. "For the first time on our screens," commented critic C. A. Lejeune, "we have the British equivalent of a Clark Gable . . . playing in a purely national idiom."

His success continued with another beauty, *The Ghost Goes West,* 1936. René Clair directed, and Donat played the dual role—as the current owner of an ancestral palace and its ghostly inhabitant from centuries past—with great skill. He next wanted to do another Hitchcock, *Sabotage,* but instead did a film Korda had bought for him, *Knight Without Armor,* 1937, an unabsorbing saga of the Russian Revolution that co-starred Marlene Dietrich.

His vacillation was his undoing. Warner Brothers counted on bringing him to the United States to make films like *Anthony Adverse* and *British Agent,* but he never arrived. Instead Metro finally signed him up. In England, he made for Metro two big successes, the screen adaptation of A. J. Cronin's *The Citadel,* 1938, and the leading tear-jerker of the period, *Goodbye, Mr. Chips,* 1939.

Knight Without Armor *(1932, United Artists, Alexander Korda)*

The Ghost Goes West *(1936, Gaumont-British)*

Goodbye, Mr. Chips *(1939, M-G-M) with Terry Kilburn*

The Citadel *(1938, M-G-M) with Rosalind Russell*

The Scarlet Pimpernel (1935, United Artists, Alexander Korda) with Merle Oberon

Leslie Howard (1893–1943)

Leslie Howard enjoyed a series of stage successes in both London and New York before going to Hollywood for his screen debut in *Outward Bound*, 1930. His performance, the recreation of his 1925 stage role, was so impressive that he was immediately cast opposite some of Hollywood's top female stars, making *Devotion*, 1931, and *The Animal Kingdom*, 1932, with Ann Harding; *A Free Soul*, 1931, and *Smilin' Through*, 1932, with Norma Shearer; and *Secrets*, 1933, with Mary Pickford.

Howard was a master at portraying sensitive, introspective and cultured gentlemen and richly deserved the critical praise and enthusiastic box-office response he received for his performances in films like *Berkeley Square*, 1933. However, in *Of Human Bondage*, 1934, and *The Petrified Forest*, 1936, starring opposite Bette Davis, he overstepped his mark and almost descended into bathos. Even so, he was reviewed favorably, and the films did nothing to injure his now established name.

Though he certainly proved himself capable of creditable dramatic performances, it was in comedy that Howard excelled. His simpering fop, Sir Percy Blakeney, in *The Scarlet Pimpernel* was a delightful characterization of a courageous man who masquerades as a dull-witted popinjay. He was wildly zany as Bette Davis' acting partner and would-be husband in *It's Love I'm After*, 1937, and his Henry Higgins in *Pygmalion*, 1938, was so much more than a misanthrope or misogynist that he made audiences want to believe that he and Eliza (Wendy Hiller) marry.

Despite his comedic success, the public seemed to prefer his playing sentimental, romantic heroes and joyously welcomed his sensitive portrayals in *Gone with the Wind*, 1939, and *Intermezzo*, 1939, his final Hollywood ventures. When World War II began, Howard returned to England, where he worked for the war effort by making patriotic films and by visiting Spain and Portugal, ostensibly to lecture on the theater. Returning from Portugal in 1943, he died, like one of his film heroes, when his plane was shot down by the Germans, who mistakenly thought Winston Churchill was aboard.

Pygmalion (1938, M-G-M) with Scott Sunderland and Wendy Hiller

Berkeley Square (1933, Fox) with Heather Angel

Intermezzo (1939, United Artists, Selznick International) with Ingrid Bergman

170

Bette Davis (1908–)

The Big Shakedown *(1934, Warner Brothers)*

Her real name was Ruth Elizabeth Davis. In 1930, at the age of 21, she flunked her first screen test. In 1938 she was Queen of Hollywood. Landing that title had not been easy.

She struggled through her first 21 films (most of them under contract to Warner Brothers), desperately trying with rotten scripts to lend credibility to an assortment of spoiled society dames, secretaries, sales clerks and models. In each, her acting ability mattered about as much as the color of her hair. Not until she was loaned to RKO-Radio Pictures was she able to demonstrate the scope, the power of her talent and personality. The picture was *Of Human Bondage,* 1934. (See pages 60-61.)

Her own studio continued to offer her impossible scripts. They forced her into five pedestrian dramas in which she played a housewife, gal reporter (twice), an alcoholic and a murderess with equal gusto and intelligence. For *Dangerous,* 1935, she won her first Oscar. Then came *The Petrified Forest,* 1936 (see pages 108-109), followed by two horrendous pictures. Davis defiantly broke her contract and sailed to England.

Davis was taken to court and lost. Still, she had maintained her integrity and forced the studio to acknowledge her unique talents. When she returned to Hollywood it was to play roles that were tailor-made for her. She earned a second Oscar for *Jezebel,* 1938 (see pages 138-139), and during the next two years starred in five of the more memorable films ever produced by Warner Brothers: *The Sisters,* 1938, *Dark Victory,* 1939, *Juarez,* 1939, *The Old Maid,* 1939, and *The Private Lives of Elizabeth and Essex,* 1939 (see pages 180-181).

Miss Davis always acted with an enormous charge of energy, scaling her characters much larger than life-size. And there were always mannerisms: the staccato, shrill-edged voice; the distinctive accent; the ever-active hands; the abrupt, jerky gait. Consequently, at the peak of her success, the mannerisms often carried her into caricature. To a modern viewer, the Queen of Hollywood, 1938, might seem more eccentric than grand.

Bordertown *(1935, Warner Brothers)*

Dark Victory *(1939, Warner Brothers)* with Humphrey Bogart and Geraldine Fitzgerald

Juarez *(1939, Warner Brothers)*

Union Pacific (1939)

"It's a socko spec, sure-fire for big grosses right down the line," *The Weekly Variety* reported, May 3, 1939. Cecil B. De Mille's *Union Pacific* was, like most of his movies, a box-office bonanza. Yet it did nothing to alter De Mille's reputation with many critics as a promising silent-era director who became little more than a third-rate purveyor of historically distorted, paper-doll epics. Like his other films, *Union Pacific* is characterized by a personal flamboyance and a staunch disregard for fact.

Its historical inaccuracies aside, the film is an exciting adventure replete with a cast led by stars and followed by a list of what seems to be Hollywood's most recognizable supporting and character actors—Regis Toomey, J. M. Kerrigan, Fuzzy Knight, Lon Chaney, Jr., Joe Sawyer, Joseph Crehan, Russell Hicks. It is a fast-paced story about the construction of the transcontinental railroad. Two rival companies are working against each other toward completion, and therein lies the conflict. Joel McCrea works for one company and his old friend Robert Preston works for the other. Not only that, Preston is married to the woman McCrea loves, Barbara Stanwyck. All is resolved when Preston is killed in an Indian attack *cum* train crash, and McCrea gets Miss Stanwyck and the tracks down in the end. That fateful train wreck deserves mention. It is one of the most ridiculous spectacles ever, with its mangled boxcars, bleeding and dead passengers, plus a band of Indians whooping it up orgiastically over the unrolling of bolts of white fabric. Symbolism, De Mille style!

Barbara Stanwyck as Mollie Monahan and Joel McCrea as Jeff Butler

Joel McCrea after one of his tussles with railroad men

Barbara Stanwyck and Robert Preston as Dick Allen

172

Robert Preston, Joel McCrea and Brian Donlevy

Joel McCrea uses the stock of his rifle as a weapon, trying to protect Robert Preston and Barbara Stanwyck

The Women (1939)

Ballyhooed by publicity as "the most hilarious Battle Over Men ever screened," this saga of female cattiness may, in the darkened cinema, have provoked the laughter it promised. But in a more objective light it becomes one of the most scathing indictments against the human animal, female *and* male, ever concocted.

Of course that was not M-G-M's intention. The studio designed it to clean up at the box offices, and thanks to the gullibility of 1939 audiences (and strong performances by Norma Shearer, Joan Crawford, Rosalind Russell and others) it did. Capitalizing on Clare Boothe's already smash-hit stage play, the film detailed the living-room tragedy of Mary (Shearer), an insipid, dutiful, high-society wife and mother whose marital bliss is shattered by the conniving "other woman" (Crawford) and by the energetic interference of her cloying, jealous, superficial, destructive "friends." Battered to a pulp, poor Mary is reduced by the final scene to a toy wife. "Pride is a luxury that a woman in love can't afford!" she says radiantly as she extends her arms toward her off-camera husband, having gone full circle from happy marriage, to betrayal, to confrontation with rival, to divorce, to a mindless reconciliation with hubby.

It is a disquieting fact that audiences didn't recoil at witnessing women reduced to a herd of vile, frivolous, pampered tarantulas and didn't object to men (not one appeared on screen to so much as register a protest!) so debased that their only value was as pawns for women's whims. Hopefully, today this sort of claptrap would be regarded by audiences as period-novelty at best and, at worst, as an insult to the intellect as well as to the sensibilities.

Joan Fontaine, Ann Morriss and Rosalind Russell

Rosalind Russell smiles as Norma Shearer admires her diamond

Lucile Watson, Virginia Weidler and Norma Shearer

174

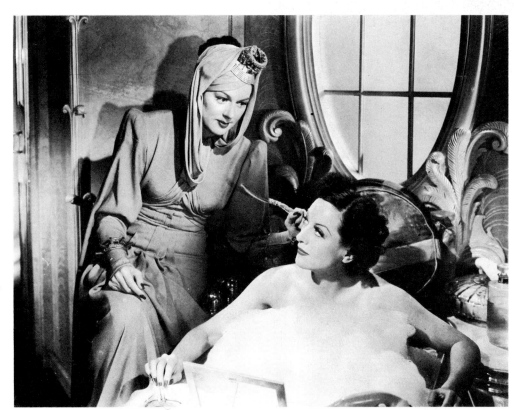

Rosalind Russell and Joan Crawford have a heart-to-heart amid bubbles

Norma Shearer, Joan Fontaine, Rosalind Russell, Paulette Goddard and Mary Boland during a ''girlish'' confrontation

Tyrone Power as Jesse James and Nancy Kelly as his gal, Zee

Jesse James (1939)

Tyrone Power starred in the title role and with the help of screenwriter Nunnally Johnson distorted history so winningly that the film was a huge success. One of the earliest Westerns filmed in Technicolor, *Jesse James* gave the already vastly popular Power the chance to let his acting talent gleam. The son of an earlier performer with the same name, he admirably took up the challenge. Henry Fonda was equally accomplished in a supporting role as Jesse's older brother, Frank.

Jesse James illustrates how Hollywood smooths over the rough edges of the past to come up with acceptable entertainment. The cold facts about the James gang were not obscured by Darryl F. Zanuck's production. They were indeed scoundrels, and, true to life, Jesse was assassinated in a most cowardly fashion. But there the similarity between fact and fiction ended. Director Henry King created folk heroes from these murdering rustlers and offered a romantic explanation for their antisocial behavior. Frontier America, a land of haves and have-nots, was no place for the weak or oppressed. Farmers eked out meager existences while the rail and banking interests accumulated huge fortunes. These suffering souls needed a champion, and in its beneficence Hollywood provided Jesse James and brother Frank, two Robin Hood types dedicated to helping the poor.

Little did it matter that the historical Jesse and his pompous brother were merciless gunslingers who ravaged the Kansas territory without social conscience. Audiences went to the movies to marvel at heroes and therefore weren't distressed to see the James gang so lavishly glorified. The occasional scenes of Jesse with his beloved Zee (Nancy Kelly) naturally fed public sympathies, and when Frank escapes we are prepared to sigh with relief (the convincing acting undoubtedly played a part here). Audiences were behind Power's dream of a life free of strife and Fonda's getaway, but they understood—with an irascible strand of realism—that crimes had been committed and that Hollywood was only right in having Jesse die an ignominious death.

Henry Fonda as Jesse's brother Frank

Henry Fonda in a spectacular getaway

Tyrone Power, Jane Darwell, Brian Donlevy and Henry Fonda

Stagecoach (1939)

Innumerable directors have panned the great open spaces of the Southwest seeking to capture on film the drama of the frontier. But none has succeeded like John Ford, and among his many excellent Westerns *Stagecoach* stands out like the Continental Divide.

The Apache-menaced plains of Arizona form the backdrop for Ford's adventure. Thrown together on a stagecoach and sharing a sense of impending disaster are a professional gambler and former Southern gentleman, a doctor given to drink, a devious banker, a brazen woman with a scandalous past, a pregnant, delicately upper-caste lady and a meek whiskey salesman. Rounding out the group is a sheriff searching for the Ringo Kid, the reputed outlaw.

The Dudley Nichols script wasn't really original, even in 1939. The U. S. Cavalry rescues the coach, and the Ringo Kid, after a classic street shootout, is redeemed. The young woman of questionable repute falls for the Kid's (John Wayne's) charms, and the two reinstated souls ride off into the sunset.

The prosaic plot was transformed according to Ford's dictum that plot situations are only a starting point beyond which the director must go. And go beyond them he did, with straightforward direction, magnificent location footage, crisp, fresh dialogue and excellent acting. *Stagecoach* made John Wayne a star. Claire Trevor, who was rarely given the roles she deserved, excelled as Dallas, the loose woman gone straight.

There have been other fine Westerns—*The Covered Wagon* in the silent era, *Cimmarron* in the 30s, *True Grit* (again Duke Wayne) in the 60s. But, to most aficionados, *Stagecoach* was the very best of them all, the paradigm for one of the most popular of movie genres.

The reformed floozy and the outlaw, played by Claire Trevor and John Wayne

Indians attack the stagecoach as it crosses the Arizona desert

John Wayne as the Ringo Kid and Claire Trevor as Dallas

Gunga Din (1939)

There was very little Gunga but a great deal of din in the screen adaptation of Rudyard Kipling's poetic tribute to a regimental *bhisti* (native water carrier) who died a hero's death on the northern frontier of Queen Victoria's India. A turbaned Sam Jaffe, dyed a deep sepia and clad in what appeared to be outsized Pampers, played the title role. He can be spotted now and again, grinning widely while cheerfully performing menial jobs for his British masters. But most of the film's footage is devoted to the boisterous and brawling activities of the starring players—Cary Grant, Victor McLaglen and Douglas Fairbanks, Jr. (with love interest supplied by Joan Fontaine).

The screenplay, written by Ben Hecht and Charles MacArthur, with a helping hand from William Faulkner, follows a well-worn pattern set years before, mostly notably by *Lives of a Bengal Lancer* in 1935. The British regiment, the guardian of an empire on which the sun never sets, stands between the glories of civilization and the chaos of aboriginal anarchy. Nearby, the natives are restless. In this case, the natives are Thugees (whence our word "thug"), worshippers of the bloodthirsty goddess Kali, who chant "Kill! Kill! Kill!" Eduardo Cianelli, a vastly menacing gangster in *Winterset*, 1936, masterfully plays the head priest of the cult.

At the film's end, of course, British imperialism triumphs; but poor Gunga Din, whose secret ambition in life is to be a British soldier, dies on the field of battle, attempting to warn the regiment, and gives point to the Kipling ending: "Though I've belted you an' flayed you,/ By the livin' Gawd that made you,/ You're a better man than I am, Gunga Din!" The fadeout is a full-screen shot of Gunga Din, superimposed over the columns of marching troops, wearing an honest-to-goodness British uniform.

Like *Clive of India*, 1935, and *Four Feathers*, 1939, *Gunga Din* is a period piece, appropriate only for a day when chauvinism was an acceptable word and audiences believed in the White Man's Burden. Its themes, sensibilities and social mores date the film. Its fast-paced action and rollicking stars, however, give the film longevity and make it fun to watch today.

Sam Jaffe in the title role

Joan Fontaine and Douglas Fairbanks, Jr.

Victor McLaglen, Douglas Fairbanks, Jr., and Cary Grant

Sam Jaffe, Cary Grant, Victor McLaglen, Douglas Fairbanks, Jr., and soldiers

Of Mice and Men (1939)

Of Mice and Men was the first movie with a pretitle sequence. It begins with two migrant workers, Lennie and George, fleeing a sheriff's posse. They succeed in boarding a moving freight train, and when they slide its heavy door shut, the camera remains outside. A passage from a Robert Burns poem is scrawled on the outside of the door in chalk: "The best laid schemes of mice and men gang aft a-gley; An' lea'e us nought but grief and pain, for promis'd joy." The prophetic words fade until only the title itself remains. The "scheme" of this poignant story by John Steinbeck is Lennie's and George's dream of a farm of their own where they can be at peace. These plans go very far astray when the dull-witted Lennie accidentally kills his foreman's wife. George kills Lennie to prevent his being brutalized by the bloodthirsty posse and, at the same time, destroys the dream as well.

Of Mice and Men is set in the farming country of the Monterey–Salinas area of California, not far from San Francisco, and was filmed in sepia by director-producer Lewis Milestone. The unusual brown tone of the film emphasizes the feeling of futility that is shared not only by the protagonists but by the other characters as well. Everyone, with the exception of the ranch owner, Slim, seems to personify the spiritual desolation caused by the Depression. The film's transmittal of something abstract and its nonverbal suggestion of rootlessness is wonderfully enhanced by a superb musical score composed by Aaron Copland, the distinguished American composer.

In addition to the technical excellence of the film, Burgess Meredith's small, quick George, Lon Chaney, Jr.'s, lumbering Lennie, Charles Bickford's unsympathetic Slim and Betty Field's sensitive Mae are finely etched performances.

Of Mice and Men won an Oscar nomination for best picture and, despite the sober, depressing theme, was one of the ten top money-makers of 1939.

Bob Steele and Lon Chaney, Jr.

Lon Chaney, Jr., and Betty Field

Lon Chaney, Jr., as Lennie and Burgess Meredith as George at the film's tragic climax

Betty Field and Lon Chaney, Jr.

Bette Davis as Elizabeth I

The Private Lives of Elizabeth and Essex (1939)

For her portrayal of Elizabeth I, Bette Davis shaved her hairline back to mid-skull; donned an assortment of flaming red wigs; strapped up in ruff-collared, bejeweled gowns by Orry-Kelly; and flounced about some of the grandest Warner Brothers sets ever constructed. Despite the film's bid for authenticity, it looked about as real as a Dagwood and Blondie comic strip. However, this misguided effort to film Maxwell Anderson's important, if talky, play provided delicious, tears-and-laughter fun.

In Davis's performance are displayed the complete range of excessive, idiosyncratic mannerisms that, by 1939, were fast becoming her trademark. The finger-flicking, fist-clutching gestures of Elizabeth were variations of the punctuating, air-slicing cigarette play she was perfecting in *Dark Victory*, 1939. The jaunty, elbows-jabbing-the-hips walk was never more exaggerated; and she finally had a legitimate reason for the British pronunciations of such lines as "You slimy toat" (toad) and "Let-tahs, let-tahs, you sent me let-tahs" (letters). Perhaps it was the ineptitude of her romantic co-star, Errol Flynn, that prompted her grandiose playing. By contrast to the other players, she and Flynn seemed characters lost on the set of another picture. Olivia de Havilland created a sincere and touching Lady Penelope Gray, and Nanette Fabares (later Fabray) was particularly believable as the heart-broken young Mistress Margaret Radcliffe.

In addition to the costumes and sets, the beautiful Technicolor photography of the film and the brassy, lyrical background score by Erich Wolfgang Korngold make the film worth remembering.

Bette Davis dallying with Errol Flynn as the Earl of Essex

John Sutton, Vincent Price, James Stevenson, Henry Daniell, Guy Bellis, Henry Stephenson, Bette Davis and Errol Flynn

Errol Flynn and John Sutton

Bette Davis and Errol Flynn

Bette Davis confronted by Olivia de Havilland as Lady Penelope Gray

Possessed *(1931, M-G-M) with Joan Crawford*

Clark Gable (1901–1960)

He was dubbed the King after Ed Sullivan's readers voted him "King of Hollywood" (Myrna Loy was the Queen) in a 1937 poll.

His first wife, acting coach Josephine Dillon, taught him his trade and promoted his early career. She was 16 years his senior, and their marriage lasted until 1930. Following two screen-test failures (one of them at Warner Brothers, where Darryl F. Zanuck scoffed, "His ears are too big, he looks like an ape"), he landed a small role in Pathe's Western *The Painted Desert*, 1931. Finally M-G-M took an interest, offering him a contract and part in *The Easiest Way*, 1931.

Public response was so overwhelming to a preview of *Dance, Fools, Dance*, 1931, featuring Gable and Joan Crawford, who had requested him for the film, that his villainous role was built up in retakes. Audiences were transfixed by the way he abused Norma Shearer in *A Free Soul*, 1931, but it was *Red Dust*, 1932, and its vivid love-making scene with Jean Harlow that sent him to the top. He was now M-G-M's biggest drawing card, and he appeared with each of the studio's most glamorous female stars—Garbo, Crawford, Harlow and Shearer. Acclaim did not bring him better parts, however, and he balked at the gigolo roles handed him and demanded more money. M-G-M tried to punish him by loaning him to Columbia for Frank Capra's *It Happened One Night*, 1934. It was hardly punishment. Gable and four others won Oscars.

He starred in many other highly successful films, but the classic Gable, and the film that immortalized him, is of course *Gone with the Wind*, 1939. He was so totally the embodiment of manliness to 30s audiences that author Margaret Mitchell reportedly modeled the character of Rhett Butler after him. When it was brought to the screen there was no doubt in anyone's mind that Gable *was* Rhett. With his popularity at its peak, and a second Oscar nomination, the King reigned in Hollywood for two more decades.

The White Sister *(1933, M-G-M) with Helen Hayes*

Hell Divers *(1931, M-G-M) with Wallace Beery*

The Secret Six *(1931, M-G-M) with Jean Harlow*

182

A Free Soul *(1931, M-G-M) with Norma Shearer*

No Man of Her Own *(1932, Paramount) with Carole Lombard*

Red Dust *(1932, M-G-M) with Jean Harlow*

Call of the Wild *(1935, United Artists, 20th Century) with Loretta Young*

Wuthering Heights (1939)

Wuthering Heights, the film version of Emily Brontë's novel about two passionate, jealous, neurotic lovers on the grim Yorkshire moors, was producer Samuel Goldwyn's contribution to the historical "epic" craze that characterized many of the 1939 movies. While Europe was tottering on the brink of war, Hollywood movie-makers were training their cameras away from the present toward a highly romantic, fictionalized past. *Wuthering Heights* was unadulterated escapist fare and typified the let's-look-the-other-way attitude that inspired other films like *Gone with the Wind, The Private Lives of Elizabeth and Essex, The Hunchback of Notre Dame, Gunga Din, The Three Musketeers, Juarez, The Man in the Iron Mask* and *Stagecoach.* Indeed, the only film of the late 30s that seemed concerned with contemporary matters was *Mr. Smith Goes to Washington.*

The MacArthur–Hecht screenplay, covering but one generation of the novel, was disappointing, for the story is infinitely more compelling and stirring in the pages of Miss Brontë's book. The film version is merely an overblown lovers' quarrel between moody, headstrong Heathcliff (Laurence Olivier) and his willful, selfish sweetheart Cathy (Merle Oberon), who sulk, battle and seek revenge on each other and in doing so ruin the lives of Edgar (David Niven) and Isabella (Geraldine Fitzgerald), whom they marry. Even the final, supposedly dramatic scene, in which Heathcliff carries the dying Cathy to a window for one last glimpse of their stomping grounds (in this case, a California hillside covered with imported heather), is a mimicry of a romantic/tragic moment and seemed to be created only to boost the sale of hankies.

Despite its shortcomings *Wuthering Heights* won an Academy Award nomination for itself and one for Olivier and was a box-office success. Perhaps in 1939 audiences needed a good cry without being forced to examine what they were crying about.

Merle Oberon as Cathy Earnshaw, Laurence Olivier as Heathcliffe and David Niven as Edgar

Merle Oberon and Laurence Olivier

David Niven and Merle Oberon

Flora Robson and Merle Oberon

184

Merle Oberon tries to dissuade Isabella (Geraldine Fitzgerald) from marrying Heathcliffe

Rain-soaked Merle Oberon on the moors

David Niven comforts the ailing Merle Oberon

Merle Oberon with Laurence Olivier shortly before her death

Angel (1937, Paramount) with Marlene Dietrich and director Ernst Lubitsch

Ernst Lubitsch (1892–1947)

Lubitsch was already an accomplished director of raucous comedies and historical spectaculars in his native Berlin before arriving in Hollywood in 1923. Throughout the 20s and 30s he was one of the most proficient directors of sparkling, risqué comedies. His handling of Oscar Wilde's *Lady Windemere's Fan*, 1925, *So This Is Paris*, 1926, and *The Student Prince*, 1927, was marked by a careful attention to style and manners and a chic, sophisticated approach to sex and comedy that earned his technique the name "The Lubitsch Touch."

Many directors copied his titillating method of sending his characters behind closed doors after suggestive glances and verbal teasing so as to suggest to audiences that scandalous doings were afoot. However, they were only grazing the surface of the Lubitsch style. They missed the brittle, sardonic edge which always attended his humor, the sadness that belied much of the bright, gay appearances of things.

His first sound picture was a musical, *The Love Parade*, 1929, which paired Jeanette MacDonald and Maurice Chevalier for the first time. A resounding success, it was followed by several others—*Monte Carlo*, 1930, *The Smiling Lieutenant*, 1931, *One Hour with You*, 1932—before MacDonald and Chevalier were reunited with Lubitsch in *The Merry Widow*, 1934. He directed segments of two films—*Paramount on Parade*, 1930, and *If I Had a Million*, 1932—and pioneered screwball comedy with the hilarious love triangles of *Trouble in Paradise*, 1932, *Design for Living*, 1933, and *Angel*, 1937. This latter film featured Marlene Dietrich in one of her finest performances. Earlier in the decade he directed an antiwar drama, *The Man I Killed*, 1932, but comedy remained his forte, as he demonstrated with his final film of the 30s, *Ninotchka*, 1939, starring Greta Garbo.

Trouble in Paradise (1932, Paramount) with Miriam Hopkins and Herbert Marshall

Bluebeard's Eighth Wife (1938, Paramount) with Gary Cooper and Claudette Colbert

186

Gladys George (1900–1954)

Though she had been in show business since the age of three and had made several silent films, Gladys George did not achieve stardom until she was thirty-six. She was neither pretty nor distinctive enough to compete with glamour girls. Her success was based on one simple ingredient: talent. She had the uncanny ability to reveal the inner qualities of a character, penetrating the outer defenses and getting at the true personality. Her women could appear sinful, but one knew that they were not really bad; they were victims. She infused her creations with intelligence and emotional depth.

If for only one film, *Valiant Is the Word for Carrie,* 1936, Miss George deserves to be remembered as one of the most poignant, sensitive actresses of the 30s. Her characterization of the disreputable Carrie, whose heart is captured by two orphans, earned critical accolades, an Oscar nomination and left none but the most hard-boiled cynics dry-eyed. She epitomized every dame who has been knocked around (brassy on the outside) but who keeps on fighting (all heart underneath).

After Carrie, Miss George starred as *Madame X,* 1937, the fourth remake of the durable sudser in which Ruth Chatterton had played so well in 1929. George's performance had such strength, such a profound sense of pathos, that even Chatterton's paled in comparison. Miss George's warm, heart-rending Jacqueline dignified the implausible, melodramatic script and made it seem believable.

Two years and five pictures later, George all but stole the picture from James Cagney in *The Roaring Twenties*. Playing a tough lady of the underworld with a heart of gold, she created one of the most memorable moments in film history when, in the final shot, she sits cradling Cagney's dead body in her arms and makes the observation, "He used to be a big shot."

Valiant Is the Word for Carrie *(1936, Paramount) with orphans*

Valiant Is the Word for Carrie *with Harry Carey*

Madame X *(1937, M-G-M) with John Beal*

Madame X *(1937, M-G-M) with Philip Reed*

Robert Montgomery (1904–   )

An aspiring writer, an accomplished actor and a thoughtful man who maintained his own ideas and values, Robert Montgomery spent a good part of the 30s battling with the ineffable Louis B. Mayer. If he hadn't been so talented M-G-M would cheerfully have exiled him to Siberia, as Montgomery's fights for more money and decent roles became legendary.

After a brief stage career and a name change (from Henry Montgomery, Jr.) he appeared in a few of the early talkies. His first major roles were opposite Norma Shearer in *Their Own Desire*, 1930, and in *The Divorcee*, 1930. Thereafter, he was almost always cast as a sleek, handsome, upper-class playboy. A typical Montgomery role, again with Shearer, was one of the quartet in Noel Coward's *Private Lives*. Here, though, he was given the chance to show his considerable comic flair for the first time.

Montgomery starred with Helen Hayes in three films: *Another Language*, 1933, *Night Flight*, 1933, and *Vanessa, Her Love Story*, 1935. There were other romantic roles as well, with Marion Davies, Madge Evans and Anita Page. Meanwhile, he turned down the Gable role in *It Happened One Night*, 1934, and the Franchot Tone part in *Mutiny on the Bounty*, 1935.

In *The Big House*, 1930, Montgomery had proved that he could be a silky killer. Seven years later he reiterated his versatility in *Night Must Fall* with his role of Danny, the psychotic murderer who carries a human head about with him in a hatbox. His final film of the decade was *Fast and Loose*, 1939.

Montgomery was active in the organization of the Screen Actors Guild and was named president in 1939. (This activity contributed to the animosity M-G-M held for him.) When Willie Bioff, one of the nation's leading gangsters, began to muscle into the film industry Montgomery hired detectives with a $5,000 fund provided by the Guild. He turned his findings over to Westbrook Pegler, whose articles sent Bioff to prison and won the Pulitzer Prize for Pegler.

Blondie of the Follies *(1932, M-G-M) with* Marion Davies

Private Lives *(1931, M-G-M) with Norma Shearer*

Love in the Rough *(1930, M-G-M) with* Dorothy Jordan

188

FILMS, CASTS AND CREDITS

TOL'ABLE DAVID

Columbia   1930
65 minutes   black and white   sound

From the story by *Joseph Hergesheimer*
Screenplay, *Benjamin Glazer*
Director, *John George Blystone*
Producer, *Harry Cohn*

CAST

David Kinemon, *Richard Cromwell;* Luke, *Noah Beery;* Mrs. Kinemon, *Helen Ware;* Esther Hatburn, *Joan Peers;* Alan Kinemon, *George Duryea;* Amos Hatburn, *Henry B. Walthall*

ALL QUIET ON THE WESTERN FRONT

Universal   1930
140 minutes   black and white   sound

From the novel by *Erich Maria Remarque*
Screenplay, *Maxwell Anderson, Dell Andrews* and *George Abbott*
Director, *Lewis Milestone*
Producer, *Carl Laemmle, Jr.*

CAST

Katczinsky, *Louis Wolheim;* Paul Baumer, *Lewis Ayres;* Himmelstoss, *John Wray;* Tjaden, *George (Slim) Summerville;* Kemmerich, *Ben Alexander;* Muller, *Russell Gleason;* Albert, *William Bakewell*

ACADEMY AWARDS: best picture; best direction, *Lewis Milestone*

MOROCCO

Paramount   1930
97 minutes   black and white   sound

From the play *Amy Jolly* by *Benno Vigny*
Adaptation (scenario and dialogue), *Jules Furthman*
Director, *Josef von Sternberg*
Producer, *Josef von Sternberg*

CAST

Tom Brown, *Gary Cooper;* Amy Jolly, *Marlene Dietrich;* Kennington, *Adolphe Menjou;* Adjutant Caesar, *Ulrich Haupt;* Anna Dolores, *Juliette Compton*

ACADEMY AWARDS NOMINATION: best actress, *Marlene Dietrich*

THE SPOILERS

Paramount   1930
84 minutes   black and white   sound

From the book by *Rex Beach*
Screenplay, *Bartlett Cormack* and *Agnes Brand Leahy*
Director and producer, *Edwin Carewe*

CAST

Glenister, *Gary Cooper;* Helen Chester, *Kay Johnson;* Cherry Malotte, *Betty Compson;* McNamara, *William Boyd;* Herman, *Harry Green;* Flapjack Slims, *Slim Summerville*

LITTLE CAESAR

Warner Brothers–First National   1930
80 minutes   black and white   sound

From the novel by *W. R. Burnett*
Adaptation (scenario and dialogue), *Francis Faragoh*
Director, *Mervyn LeRoy*
Producer, *Jack L. Warner*

CAST

Caesar Enrico Bandello, *Edward G. Robinson;* Joe Massara, *Douglas Fairbanks, Jr.;* Olga Strassoff, *Glenda Farrell;* Tony Passa, *William Collier, Jr.;* Diamond Pete Montana, *Ralph Ince;* The Big Boy, *Sidney Blackmer*

THE PUBLIC ENEMY

Warner Brothers–Vitaphone   1931
84 minutes   black and white   sound

From the story by *Kubec Glasmon* and *John Bright*
Adaptation, *Harvey Thew*
Director, *William Wellman*
Producer, *Kubec Glasmon*

CAST

Tom Powers, *James Cagney;* Matt Doyle, *Edward Woods;* Mike Powers, *Donald Cook;* Mamie, *Joan Blondell;* Gwen Allen, *Jean Harlow;* Kitty, *Mae Clark;* Mrs. Powers, *Beryl Mercer*

CITY LIGHTS

Charles Chaplin–United Artists   1931
87 minutes   black and white   silent with synchronized sound

From a story by *Charles Chaplin*
Director and producer, *Charles Chaplin*
Original music, *Charles Chaplin*

CAST

A Blind Girl, *Virginia Cherrill;* Her Grandmother, *Florence Lee;* An Eccentric Millionaire, *Harry Myers;* His Butler, *Alan Garcia;* A Prizefighter, *Hank Mann;* A Tramp, *Charles Chaplin*

CIMARRON

RKO   1931
130 minutes   black and white   sound

From the novel by *Edna Ferber*
Adaptation (scenario and dialogue), *Howard Estabrook*
Director and producer, *Wesley Ruggles*

CAST

Yancy Cravat, *Richard Dix;* Sabra Cravat, *Irene Dunne;* Dixie Lee, *Estelle Taylor;* Felice Venable, *Nance O' Neil;* The Kid, *William Collier, Jr.;* Jess Rickey, *Roscoe Ates;* Sol Levy, *George E. Stone;* Mrs. Tracy Wyatt, *Edna May Oliver;* Bit actor, *Dennis O'Keefe*

ACADEMY AWARDS: best picture; best art direction, *Max Ree;* best writing, adaptation, *Howard Estabrook*

ACADEMY AWARDS NOMINATIONS: best actor, *Richard Dix;* best actress, *Irene Dunne*

BIRD OF PARADISE

RKO   1932
80 minutes   black and white   sound

From the play by *Richard Walton Tully*
Screenplay, *Wells Root*
Director, *King Vidor*
Producer, *David O. Selznick*

CAST

Luana, *Dolores Del Rio;* Johnny Baker, *Joel McCrea;* Mac, *John Halliday;* Thornton, *Creighton Chaney* (later, *Lon Chaney, Jr.*); Chester, *Richard ''Skeets'' Gallagher*

GRAND HOTEL

M-G-M   1932
115 minutes   black and white   sound

From the novel and play by *Vicki Baum*
Adaptation, *William A. Drake*
Director, *Edmund Goulding*
Producer, *Irving Thalberg*

CAST

Grusinskaya, *Greta Garbo;* Flaemmchen, *Joan Crawford;* Preysing, *Wallace Beery;* Baron Felix von Geigern, *John Barrymore;* Otto Kringelein, *Lionel Barrymore;* Dr. Otternschlag, *Lewis Stone;* Senf, *Jean Hersholt;* Pimenov, *Ferdinand Gottschalk*

ACADEMY AWARDS: best picture

CAVALCADE

Fox   1933
109 minutes   black and white   sound

From the play by *Noel Coward*
Adaptation and dialogue, *Reginald Berkeley*
Director, *Frank Lloyd*
Producer, *Winfield Sheehan*
Song ''Twentieth Century Blues,'' *Noel Coward*

CAST

Robert Marryot, *Clive Brook;* Jane Marryot, *Diana Wynyard;* Fanny Bridges, *Ursula Jeans;* Alfred Brudges, *Herbert Mundin;* Ellen Bridges, *Una O'Connor;* Joe Marryot, *Frank Lawton;* Edward Marryot, *John Warburton;* Annie, *Merle Tottenham;* Margaret Harris, *Irene Browne;* Cook, *Beryl Mercer;* George Grainger, *Billy Bevan;* Fanny at 7–12, *Bonita Granville;* Girl on couch, *Betty Grable*

ACADEMY AWARDS: best picture; best director, *Frank Lloyd;* best art direction, *William S. Darling*

ACADEMY AWARDS NOMINATION: best actress, *Diana Wynyard*

LITTLE WOMEN

RKO   1933
107 minutes (cut from 115 minutes)   black and white   sound

From the novel by *Louisa May Alcott*
Screenplay, *Sarah Y. Mason* and *Victor Heerman*
Director, *George Cukor*
Executive producer, *Merian C. Cooper*

CAST

Jo, *Katharine Hepburn;* Amy, *Joan Bennett;* Fritz Bhaer, *Paul Lukas;* Meg, *Frances Dee;* Beth, *Jean Parker;* Aunt March, *Edna May Oliver;* Laurie, *Douglass Montgomery;* Mr. Laurence, *Henry Stephenson;* Marmee, *Spring Byington;* Brooks, *John Davis Lodge*

ACADEMY AWARDS: best adaptation, *Sarah Y. Mason* and *Victor Heerman*

ACADEMY AWARDS NOMINATION: best picture

DINNER AT EIGHT

M-G-M   1933
113 minutes   black and white   sound

From the play by *George S. Kaufman* and *Edna Ferber*
Screenplay, *Frances Marion* and *Herman J. Mankiewicz*
Director, *George Cukor*
Producer, *David O. Selznick*

CAST

Larry Renault, *John Barrymore;* Kitty Packard, *Jean Harlow;* Oliver Jordan, *Lionel Barrymore;* Millicent Jordan, *Billie Burke;* Dan Packard, *Wallace Beery;* Wayne Talbot, *Edmond Lowe;* Carlotta Vance, *Marie Dressler;* Max Kane, *Lee Tracy;* Paula Jordan, *Madge Evans;* Hattie Loomis, *Louise Closser Hale;* Cook, *May Robson;* Miss Copeland, *Elizabeth Patterson*

DESIGN FOR LIVING

Paramount   1933
95 minutes   black and white   sound

Based on the play by *Noel Coward*
Scenarist, *Ben Hecht*
Director and producer, *Ernst Lubitsch*

CAST

Tom Chambers, *Fredric March;* George Curtis, *Gary Cooper;* Gilda Farrell, *Miriam Hopkins;* Max Plunkett, *Edward Everett Horton;* Mr. Douglas, *Franklin Pangborn*

TWENTIETH CENTURY

Columbia   1934
91 minutes   black and white   sound

Based on the play by *Ben Hecht* and *Charles MacArthur,* adapted from the play *Napoleon of Broadway* by *Charles Bruce Milholland*
Screenplay, *Ben Hecht* and *Charles MacArthur*
Director, *Howard Hawks*

CAST

Oscar Jaffe, *John Barrymore;* Lilly Garland (Mildred Plotka), *Carole Lombard;* Owen O'Malley, *Roscoe Karns;* Oliver Webb, *Walter Connolly;* George Smith, *Ralph Forbes;* Sadie, *Dale Fuller;* Matthew J. Clark, *Etienne Girardot*

THE HOUSE OF ROTHSCHILD

United Artists   1934
86 minutes   Last sequence in Technicolor   sound

From an unproduced play by *George Hembert Westley*
Screenplay, *Nunnally Johnson*
Director, *Alfred Werker*
Producer, *Darryl F. Zanuck*

CAST

Mayer Rothschild/Nathan Rothschild, *George Arliss;* Count Ledrantz, *Boris Karloff;* Julie Rothschild, *Loretta Young;* Captain Fitzroy, *Robert Young;* Duke of Wellington, *C. Aubrey Smith;* Baring, *Arthur Byron;* Gudula Rothschild, *Helen Westley;* Herries, *Reginald Owen;* Hannah Rothschild, *Florence Arliss;* Metternich, *Alan Mowbray*

ACADEMY AWARDS NOMINATION: best picture

THE LOST PATROL

RKO 1934
74 minutes   black and white   sound

From a story by *Philip MacDonald*
Adaptation, *Garrett Fort*
Screenplay, *Dudley Nichols*
Director, *John Ford*

CAST

Sergeant, *Victor McLaglen*; Sanders, *Boris Karloff*; Morelli, *Wallace Ford*; Brown, *Reginald Denny*; Quincannon, *J. M. Kerrigan*; Hale, *Billy Bevan*; Cook, *Alan Hale*

IT HAPPENED ONE NIGHT

Columbia 1934
105 minutes   black and white   sound

From a story by *Samuel Hopkins Adams*
Screenplay, *Robert Riskin*
Director, *Frank Capra*
Producer, *Harry Cohn*

CAST

Peter Warne, *Clark Gable*; Ellie Andrews, *Claudette Colbert*; Alexander Andrews, *Walter Connolly*; Oscar Shapely, *Roscoe Karns*; Danker, *Alan Hale*; Bus driver, *Ward Bond*

ACADEMY AWARDS: best picture; best actor, *Clark Gable*; best actress, *Claudette Colbert*; best director, *Frank Capra*; best adaptation, *Robert Riskin*

OF HUMAN BONDAGE

RKO 1934
83 minutes   black and white   sound

From the novel by *Somerset Maugham*
Screenplay, *Lester Cohen*
Director, *John Cromwell*
Producer, *Pandro S. Berman*

CAST

Philip Carey, *Leslie Howard*; Mildred Rogers, *Bette Davis*; Miller, *Alan Hale*; Nora, *Kay Johnson*; Sally, *Frances Dee*; Griffiths, *Reginald Denny*; Athelny, *Reginald Owen*

THE LAST DAYS OF POMPEII

RKO 1935
96 minutes   black and white   sound

Based on the novel by *Bulwer-Lytton*
Screenplay, *Ruth Rose* and *Boris Ingster*
Director, *Ernest B. Schoedsack*
Producer, *Merian C. Cooper*

CAST

Marcus, *Preston Foster*; Pontius Pilate, *Basil Rathbone*; Flavius, *David Holt*; Prefect of Pompeii, *Louis Calhern*

A MIDSUMMER NIGHT'S DREAM

Warner Brothers 1935
132 minutes   black and white   sound

From the play by *William Shakespeare*
Screenplay, *Charles Kenyon* and *Mary McCall, Jr.*
Directors, *Max Reinhardt* and *William Dieterle*
Producer, *Max Reinhardt*

CAST

Bottom, *James Cagney*; Lysander, *Dick Powell*; Flute, *Joe E. Brown*; Helena, *Jean Muir*; Snout, *Hugh Herbert*; Theseus, *Ian Hunter*; Quince, *Frank McHugh*; Oberon, *Victor Jory*; Hermia, *Olivia de Havilland*; Titania, *Anita Louise*; Puck, *Mickey Rooney*; Ninny's Tomb, *Arthur Treacher*

ACADEMY AWARDS: best film editing, *Bill Dawson*; best cinematography, *Hal Mohr*

ACADEMY AWARDS NOMINATION: best picture

CAPTAIN BLOOD

Warner Brothers 1935
119 minutes   black and white   sound

From the novel by *Rafael Sabatini*
Screenplay, *Casey Robinson*
Director, *Michael Curtiz*
Producer, *Hal B. Wallis*

CAST

Peter Blood, *Errol Flynn*; Arabella Bishop, *Olivia de Havilland*; Colonel Bishop, *Lionel Atwill*; Captain Levasseur, *Basil Rathbone*; Jeremy Pitt, *Ross Alexander*; Hagthorpe, *Guy Kibbee*

ACADEMY AWARDS NOMINATION: best picture

THE INFORMER

RKO 1935
91 minutes   black and white   sound

From the book by *Liam O'Flaherty*
Screenplay, *Dudley Nichols*
Director, *John Ford*
Producer, *Cliff Reid*

CAST

Gypo Nolan, *Victor McLaglen*; Mary McPhillip, *Heather Angel*; Dan Gallagher, *Preston Foster*; Katie Madden, *Margot Grahame*; Frankie McPhillip, *Wallace Ford*; Mrs. McPhillip, *Una O'Connor*; Peter Mulligan, *Donald Meek*; Flynn, *Francis Ford*

ACADEMY AWARDS: best actor, *Victor McLaglen*; best director, *John Ford*

ACADEMY AWARDS NOMINATION: best picture

MUTINY ON THE BOUNTY

M-G-M 1935
132 minutes   black and white   sound

From the book by *Charles Nordhoff* and *James Norman Hall*
Screenplay, *Talbot Jennings, Jules Furthman* and *Carey Wilson*
Director, *Frank Lloyd*
Producer, *Irving Thalberg*

CAST

Captain Bligh, *Charles Laughton*; Fletcher Christian, *Clark Gable*; Roger Byam, *Franchot Tone*; Tehani, *Movita*; Miamiti, *Mamo Clark*; Burkitt, *Donald Crisp*; Ellison, *Eddie Quillan*; Mrs. Byam, *Spring Byington*

ACADEMY AWARDS: best picture

ACADEMY AWARDS NOMINATION: best actor, *Clark Gable, Charles Laughton*

CAMILLE

M-G-M 1936
108 min   black and white   sound

From the play and novel *La Dame aux Camellias* by *Alexandre Dumas*
Screenplay, *Zoë Akins, Frances Marion* and *James Hilton*
Director, *George Cukor*

CAST

Marguerite Gautier, *Greta Garbo*; Armand, *Robert Taylor*; General Duval, *Lionel Barrymore*; Baron de Varville, *Henry Daniell*; Nichette, *Elizabeth Allan*; Olympe, *Lenore Ulric*; Prudence, *Laura Hope Crews*; Nanine, *Jessie Ralph*; Gaston, *Rex O'Malley*

THE GREAT ZIEGFELD

M-G-M 1936
184 minutes   black and white   sound

Story and screenplay, *William Anthony McGuire*
Director, *Robert Z. Leonard*
Producer, *Hunt Stromberg*
Musical director, *Arthur Lange*

CAST

Flo Ziegfeld, *William Powell*; Anna Held, *Luise Rainer*; Billie Burke, *Myrna Loy*; Billings, *Frank Morgan*; Sampston, *Reginald Owen*; Sandow, *Nat Pendleton*; Audrey Lane, *Virginia Bruce*; Fannie Brice, *herself*; Ray Bolger, *himself*; Singer, *Stanley Morner (Dennis Morgan)*

ACADEMY AWARDS: best picture; best actress, *Luise Rainer*; best dance direction, *Seymour Felix*

SAN FRANCISCO

M-G-M 1936
115 minutes   black and white   sound

From a story by *Robert Hopkins*
Screenplay, *Anita Loos*
Director, *W. S. Van Dyke*
Producers, *John Emerson* and *Bernard H. Hyam*
Song "San Francisco" by *Gus Kahn* and *B. Kaper*

CAST

Blackie Norton, *Clark Gable*; Mary Blake, *Jeanette MacDonald*; Father Tim Mullin, *Spencer Tracy*; John Burley, *Jack Holt*; Mat, *Ted Healy*; Della, *Margaret Irving*

ACADEMY AWARDS: best sound recording

ACADEMY AWARDS NOMINATIONS: best picture; best actor, *Spencer Tracy*

THE PLAINSMAN

Paramount 1936
113 minutes   black and white   sound

From stories by *Frank J. Wilstach, Courtney Ryley Cooper* and *Grover Jones*
Adaptation, *Jeanie MacPherson*
Producer and director, *Cecil B. De Mille*

CAST

Wild Bill Hickok, *Gary Cooper*; Calamity Jane, *Jean Arthur*; Buffalo Bill Cody, *James Ellison*; John Latimer, *Charles Bickford*; Jack McCall, *Porter Hall*; Louisa Cody, *Helen Burgess*; Yellow Hand, *Paul Harvey*; Painted Horse, *Victor Varconi*; Custer, *John Miljan*; Cheyenne brave, *Anthony Quinn*; Bit player, *Bud Flanagan (Dennis O'Keefe)*

ROMEO AND JULIET

M-G-M 1936
127 minutes   black and white   sound

From the play by *William Shakespeare*
Director, *George Cukor*
Producer, *Irving Thalberg*

CAST

Juliet, *Norma Shearer*; Romeo, *Leslie Howard*; Nurse, *Edna May Oliver*; Mercutio, *John Barrymore*; Lord Capulet, *C. Aubrey Smith*; Tybalt, *Basil Rathbone*; Peter, *Andy Devine*; Benvolio, *Reginald Denny*

ACADEMY AWARDS NOMINATIONS: best picture; best actress, *Norma Shearer*

THE PETRIFIED FOREST

Warner Brothers–First National 1936
83 minutes   black and white   sound

From the play by *Robert E. Sherwood*
Screenplay, *Charles Kenyon*
Director, *Archie Mayo*
Producer, *Henry Blanke*

CAST

Alan Squire, *Leslie Howard*; Gabby Maple, *Bette Davis*; Duke Mantee, *Humphrey Bogart*; Mrs. Chisholm, *Genevieve Tobin*; Boze Hertzlinger, *Dick Foran*; Gramps, *Charlie Grapewin*; Jackie, *Joseph Sawyer*; Jason Maple, *Porter Hall*

ANTHONY ADVERSE

Warner Brothers 1936
136 minutes   black and white   sound

From the novel by *Hervey Allen*
Screenplay, *Sheridan Gibney*
Director, *Mervyn LeRoy*
Producer, *Jack L. Warner*

CAST

Anthony Adverse, *Fredric March*; Angela Guisseppi, *Olivia de Havilland*; Maria, *Anita Louise*; John Bonnyfeather, *Edmund Gwenn*; Don Luis, *Claude Rains*; Vincente Nolte, *Donald Woods*; Dennis Moore, *Louis Hayward*; Faith, *Gale Sondergaard*; Carlo Cibo, *Akim Tamiroff*; Tony Guisseppi, *Luis Alberni*; Anthony's son, *Scotty Beckett*

ACADEMY AWARDS: supporting actress, *Gale Sondergaard*; cinematography, *Tony Gaudio*; film editing, *Ralph Dawson*; musical score, *Leo Forbstein*; music director; *Erich Korngold*, composer

ACADEMY AWARDS NOMINATION: best picture

THE GOOD EARTH

M-G-M 1937
138 minutes   black and white (tinted sepia)   sound

From the novel by *Pearl S. Buck*
Screenplay, *Talbot Jennings, Tess Schlesinger, Claudine West*
Director, *Sidney Franklin*
Producer, *Irving Thalberg*

CAST

Wang, *Paul Muni*; O-lan, *Luise Rainer*; Uncle, *Walter Connolly*; Lotus, *Tillie Losch*; Cuckoo, *Jessie Ralph*; Old Father, *Charles Grapewin*; Elder Son, *Keye Luke*; Bit player, *Richard Loo*

ACADEMY AWARDS: best actress, *Luise Rainer*; cinematography, *Karl Freund*

ACADEMY AWARDS NOMINATION: best picture

DEAD END

United Artists   1937
93 minutes   black and white   sound

From the play by *Sidney Kingsley*
Screenplay, *Lillian Hellman*
Director, *William Wyler*
Producer, *Samuel Goldwyn*

CAST

Drina, *Sylvia Sidney;* Dave, *Joel McCrea;* Baby Face Martin, *Humphrey Bogart;* Kay, *Wendy Barrie;* Francie, *Claire Trevor;* Hunk, *Allen Jenkins;* Mrs. Martin, *Marjorie Main;* Tommy, *Billy Halop;* Dippy, *Huntz Hall;* Angel, *Bobby Jordan;* Spit, *Leo Gorcey;* Doorman, *Ward Bond*

ACADEMY AWARDS NOMINATION: best picture

LOST HORIZON

Columbia   1937
118 minutes   black and white   sound

From the novel by *James Hilton*
Screenplay, *Robert Riskin*
Producer and director, *Frank Capra*

CAST

Robert Conway, *Ronald Colman;* Sondra, *Jane Wyatt;* Alexander P. Lovett, *Edward Everett Horton;* George Conway, *John Howard;* Henry Banard, *Thomas Mitchell;* Maria, *Margo;* Gloria Stone, *Isabel Jewell;* Chang, *H. B. Warner;* High Lama, *Sam Jaffe;* Airport official, *Richard Loo*

ACADEMY AWARDS: best art direction, *Stephen Goosson;* best film editing, *Gene Milford, Gene Havlick*

ACADEMY AWARDS NOMINATION: best picture

THE HURRICANE

United Artists   1937
110 minutes   black and white   sound

From the novel by *Charles Nordhoff* and *James Norman Hall*
Adaptation, *Dudley Nichols* and *Oliver H. P. Garrett*
Directors, *John Ford, Stuart Heisler*
Producer, *Samuel Goldwyn*
Song "Moon of Manakoora," *Frank Loesser* and *Alfred Newman*

CAST

Marama, *Dorothy Lamour;* Terangi, *Jon Hall;* Madame De Laage, *Mary Astor;* Father Paul, *C. Aubrey Smith;* Dr. Kersaint, *Thomas Mitchell;* Governor De Laage, *Raymond Massey;* Warden, *John Carradine;* Captain Nagle, *Jerome Cowan*

ACADEMY AWARDS: sound recording, *Thomas T. Moulton*

THE PRISONER OF ZENDA

United Artists   1937
101 minutes   sepia   sound

From the novel by *Anthony J. Hope* and the play by *Edward Rose*
Screenplay, *John Ballderston, Willis Root* and *Donald Ogden Stewart*
Directors, *John Cromwell* and *W. S. Van Dyke*
Producer, *David O. Selznick*

CAST

Rudolph Rassendyl–King Rudolf V, *Ronald Colman;* Princess Flavia, *Madeleine Carroll;* Rupert of Hentzau, *Douglas Fairbanks, Jr.;* Antoinette De Mauban, *Mary Astor;* Colonel Zapt, *C. Aubrey Smith;* Black Michael, *Raymond Massey;* Captain Fritz von Tarlenheim, *David Niven;* Detchard, *Montagu Love*

THE AWFUL TRUTH

Columbia   1937
90 minutes   black and white   sound

From the play by *Arthur Richman*
Screenplay, *Viña Delmar*
Producer and director, *Leo McCarey*
Songs "My Dreams Have Gone with the Wind" and "I Don't Like Music," *Ben Oakland* and *Milton Drake*

CAST

Lucy Warriner, *Irene Dunne;* Jerry Warriner, *Cary Grant;* Daniel Leeson, *Ralph Bellamy;* Armand Duvalle, *Alexander D'Arcy;* Aunt Patsy, *Cecil Cunningham;* Barbara Vance, *Molly Lament*

ACADEMY AWARDS: best director, *Leo McCarey*

ACADEMY AWARDS NOMINATION: best picture

MARIE ANTOINETTE

M-G-M   1938
160 minutes   black and white   sound

From the book by *Stephan Zweig*
Screenplay, *Claudine West, Donald Ogden Stewart, Ernest Vajda*
Director, *W. S. Van Dyke*
Producer, *Hunt Stromberg*
Song "Amour Eternal Amour," *Bob Wright, Chet Forrest, Herbert Stothart*

CAST

Marie Antoinette, *Norma Shearer;* Count Axel de Fersen, *Tyrone Power;* King Louis XV, *John Barrymore;* Mme Du Barry, *Gladys George;* King Louis XVI, *Robert Morley;* Princess DeLamballe, *Anita Louise;* Duke of Orleans, *Joseph Schildkraut;* Dauphin, *Scotty Beckett;* Peddler, *Barry Fitzgerald*

ACADEMY AWARDS NOMINATION: best actress, *Norma Shearer*

SUEZ

20th Century–Fox   1938
104 minutes   black and white   sound

From a story by *Sam Duncan*
Screenplay, *Philip Dunne* and *Julien Josephson*
Director, *Allan Dwan*
Producer, *Darryl F. Zanuck*

CAST

Ferdinand de Lesseps, *Tyrone Power;* Countess Eugenie De Montijo, *Loretta Young;* Toni Pellerin, *Annabella;* Prince Said, *J. Edward Bromberg;* Viscomte René De Latour, *Joseph Schildkraut;* Count Mathieu de Lesseps, *Henry Stephenson;* Marquis Du Brey, *Sidney Blackmer*

JEZEBEL

Warner Brothers–First National   1938
104 minutes   black and white   sound

From the play by *Owen Davis, Sr.*
Screenplay, *Clements Ripley, Abem Finkel* and *John Huston*
Screenplay contributor, *Robert Bruckner*
Director, *William Wyler*
Producer, *Hal B. Wallis*

CAST

Julie Marston, *Bette Davis;* Pres Dillard, *Henry Fonda;* Buck Cantrell, *George Brent;* Aunt Belle, *Fay Bainter;* Ted Dillard, *Richard Cromwell;* Mrs. Kendrick, *Spring Byington*

ACADEMY AWARDS: best actress, *Bette Davis;* best supporting actress, *Fay Bainter*

ACADEMY AWARDS NOMINATION: best picture

IN OLD CHICAGO

20th Century–Fox   1938
110 minutes   black and white   sound

From the story "We the O'Learys" by *Niven Busch*
Screenplay, *Lamar Trotti* and *Sonya Levien*
Director, *Henry King*
Producer, *Darryl F. Zanuck*

CAST

Dion O'Leary, *Tyrone Power;* Belle Fawcett, *Alice Faye;* Jack O'Leary, *Don Ameche;* Molly O'Leary, *Alice Brady;* Pickle Bixby, *Andy Devine;* Gil Warren, *Brian Donlevy;* General Phil Sheridan, *Sidney Blackmer*

ACADEMY AWARDS: supporting actress, *Alice Brady;* best assistant director, *Robert Webb*

ACADEMY AWARDS NOMINATION: best picture

THE AMAZING DR. CLITTERHOUSE

Warner Brothers–First National   1938
87 minutes   black and white   sound

From the play by *Barré Lyndon*
Screenplay, *John Wexley* and *John Huston*
Director and producer, *Anatole Litvak*

CAST

Dr. Clitterhouse, *Edward G. Robinson;* Jo Keller, *Claire Trevor;* Rocks Valentine, *Humphrey Bogart;* Ollay, *Allen Jenkins;* Inspector Lane, *Donald Crisp*

YOU CAN'T TAKE IT WITH YOU

Columbia   1938
120 minutes   black and white   sound

From the play by *George S. Kaufman* and *Moss Hart*
Screenplay, *Robert Riskin*
Producer and director, *Frank Capra*

CAST

Alice Sycamore, *Jean Arthur;* Martin Vanderhof, *Lionel Barrymore;* Tony Kirby, *James Stewart;* Anthony F. Kirby, *Edward Arnold;* Kolenkov, *Mischa Auer;* Essie Carmichael, *Ann Miller;* Penny Sycamore, *Spring Byington;* Paul Sycamore, *Samuel S. Hinds;* Poppins, *Donald Meek;* Ramsey, *H. B. Warner;* Detective, *Ward Bond*

MR. SMITH GOES TO WASHINGTON

Columbia   1939
125 minutes   black and white   sound

From the story by *Lewis R. Foster*
Screenplay, *Sidney Buchman*
Producer and director, *Frank Capra*

CAST

Jefferson Smith, *James Stewart;* Saunders, *Jean Arthur;* Senator Joseph Paine, *Claude Rains;* Boss Jim Taylor, *Edward Arnold;* Governor Hopper, *Guy Kibbee;* Diz Moore, *Thomas Mitchell;* Chick McCann, *Eugene Pallette;* Ma Smith, *Beulah Bondi*

ACADEMY AWARDS NOMINATIONS: best picture; best actor, *James Stewart*

GOLDEN BOY

Columbia   1939
99 minutes   black and white   sound

From the play by *Clifford Odets*
Screenplay, *Lewis Meltzer, Daniel Taradash, Sarah Y. Maem, Victor Heerman*
Director, *Rouben Mamoulian*
Producer, *William Perlberg*

CAST

Lorna Moon, *Barbara Stanwyck;* Joe Bonaparte, *William Holden;* Tom Moody, *Adolphe Menjou;* Mr. Bonaparte, *Lee J. Cobb;* Eddie Fuseli, *Joseph Calleia;* Siggie, *Sam Levene;* Roxy Lewis, *Edward S. Brophy*

GONE WITH THE WIND

M-G-M–Selznick International   1939
225 minutes   Technicolor   sound

From the novel by *Margaret Mitchell*
Screenplay, *Sidney Howard*
Director, *Victor Fleming* (with *Sam Wood* and *George Cukor*)
Producer, *David O'Selznick*

CAST

Rhett Butler, *Clark Gable;* Scarlett O'Hara, *Vivien Leigh;* Ashley Wilkes, *Leslie Howard;* Melanie Hamilton, *Olivia de Havilland;* Gerald O'Hara, *Thomas Mitchell;* Aunt Pittypat Hamilton, *Laura Hope Crews;* Mammy, *Hattie McDaniel;* Prissy, *Butterfly McQueen;* Jonas Wilkerson, *Victor Jory;* Suellen, *Evelyn Keyes;* Careen, *Ann Rutherford;* Dolly Merriwether, *Jane Darwell;* Yankee Captain, *Ward Bond*

ACADEMY AWARDS: best picture; best actress, *Vivien Leigh;* best supporting actress, *Hattie McDaniel;* best director, *Victor Fleming;* best screenplay, *Sidney Howard;* best color cinematography, *Ernest Haller* and *Ray Rennahan;* best art direction, *Lyle Wheeler;* best film editing, *Hal C. Kern* and *James E. Newcom.* Special Oscar to William Cameron Menzies for outstanding achievement in the use of color for the enhancement of dramatic mood. Scientific and Technical Oscar to *Don Musgrave* and Selznick International Pictures, Inc., for pioneering in the use of coordinated equipment.

ACADEMY AWARDS NOMINATION: best actor, *Clark Gable*
IRVING G. THALBERG MEMORIAL AWARD, *David O. Selznick*

THE WIZARD OF OZ

M-G-M   1939
101 minutes   Technicolor, opening and closing   sound
scenes in sepia

From the book by *L. Frank Baum*
Screenplay, *Noel Langley, Florence Ryerson* and *Edgar Allan Wolfe*
Director, *Victor Fleming*
Producer, *Mervyn LeRoy*
Songs, *E. Y. Harburg* and *Harold Arlen*

CAST

Dorothy, *Judy Garland*; Professor Marvel (The Wizard), *Frank Morgan*; Hunk (Scarecrow), *Ray Bolger*; Zeke (Cowardly Lion), *Bert Lahr*; Hickory (Tin Woodman), *Jack Haley*; Glinda (the Good Witch), *Billie Burke*; Miss Gulch (the Wicked Witch of the West), *Margaret Hamilton*; Uncle Henry, *Charles Grapewin*; Nikko, *Pat Walshe*; Auntie Em, *Clara Blandick*

ACADEMY AWARDS: best original score, *Herbert Stothart*; best song, *Harold Arlen* and *E. Y. Harburg* for "Over the Rainbow"

ACADEMY AWARDS NOMINATION: best picture

THE RAINS CAME

20th Century–Fox   1939
103 minutes   black and white   sound

From the novel by *Louis Bromfield*
Screenplay, *Philip Dunne* and *Julien Josephson*
Director, *Clarence Brown*
Producer, *Darryl F. Zanuck*

CAST

Lady Edwina Esketh, *Myrna Loy*; Major Rama Safti, *Tyrone Power*; Tom Ransome, *George Brent*; Fern Simon, *Brenda Joyce*; Lord Albert Esketh, *Nigel Bruce*; Maharani, *Maria Ouspenskaya*; Mr. Bannerjee, *Joseph Schildkraut*; Aunt Phoebe, *Jane Darwell*; Mrs. Simon, *Marjorie Rambeau*; Lily Hoggett-Egbury, *Laura Hope Crews*

ACADEMY AWARDS: best special effects

THE ADVENTURES OF SHERLOCK HOLMES

20th Century–Fox   1939
82 minutes   black and white   sound

Based on the play by *William Gillette*
Screenplay, *Edwin Blum* and *William Drake*
Director, *Alfred Werker*

CAST

Sherlock Holmes, *Basil Rathbone*; Dr. Watson, *Nigel Bruce*; Ann Brandon, *Ida Lupino*; Jerrold Hunter, *Alan Marshal*; Billy, *Terry Kilburn*; Professor Moriarty, *George Zucco*; Sir Ronald Ramsgate, *Henry Stephenson*

UNION PACIFIC

Paramount   1939
135 minutes   black and white   sound

From the story by *Ernest Haycox*
Adaptation, *Jack Cunningham*
Screenplay, *Walter DeLeon, C. Gardner Sullivan* and *Jesse Lasky, Jr.*
Producer and director, *Cecil B. De Mille*

CAST

Mollie Monahan, *Barbara Stanwyck*; Jeff Butler, *Joel McCrea*; Sid Campeau, *Brian Donlevy*; Dick Allen, *Robert Preston*; Fiesta, *Akim Tamiroff*; Jack Cordray, *Anthony Quinn*; Mrs. Calvin, *Evelyn Keyes*; Paddy O'Rourke, *Regis Toomey*; Dollarhide, *Lon Chaney, Jr.*

THE WOMEN

M-G-M   1939
132 minutes   Fashion-show sequence in Technicolor   sound

From the play by *Clare Boothe*
Screenplay, *Anita Loos* and *Jane Murfin*
Director, *George Cukor*
Producer, *Hunt Stomberg*

CAST

Mary Haines, *Norma Shearer*; Chrystal Allen, *Joan Crawford*; Sylvia Fowler, *Rosalind Russell*; Countess Delave, *Mary Boland*; Miriam Aarons, *Paulette Goddard*; Peggy Day, *Joan Fontaine*; Mrs. Moorehead, *Lucile Watson*; Edith Potter, *Phyllis Povah*; Miss Watts, *Ruth Hussey*; Mrs. Wagstaff, *Margaret Dumont*; Lucy, *Marjorie Main*; Dolly, *Hedda Hopper*; Mrs. Van Adams, *Cora Witherspoon*

JESSE JAMES

20th Century–Fox   1939
105 minutes   Technicolor   sound

Original screenplay, *Nunnally Johnson*
Director, *Henry King*
Producer, *Darryl F. Zanuck*

CAST

Jesse James, *Tyrone Power*; Frank James, *Henry Fonda*; Zee, *Nancy Kelly*; Will Wright, *Randolph Scott*; Major, *Henry Hull*; Jailer, *Slim Summerville*; Runyon, *J. Edward Bromberg*; Barshee, *Brian Donlevy*; The Killer, *John Carradine*; McCoy, *Donald Meek*; Mrs. Samuels, *Jane Darwell*

STAGECOACH

United Artists   1939
99 minutes   black and white   sound

From the story by *Ernest Haycox*
Screenplay, *Dudley Nichols*
Director, *John Ford*
Producer, *Walter Wanger*

CAST

Ringo Kid, *John Wayne*; Dallas, *Claire Trevor*; Doc Boone, *Thomas Mitchell*; Hatfield, *John Carradine*; Bucky, *Andy Devine*; Mr. Peacock, *Donald Meek*; Curley Wilcox, *George Bancroft*; Lucy Mallory, *Louise Platt*; Sergeant Billy Pickett, *Francis Ford*

ACADEMY AWARDS: best supporting actor, *Thomas Mitchell*; best score, *Hageman, Harling, Leipold* and *Shuken*

ACADEMY AWARDS NOMINATION: best picture

GUNGA DIN

RKO   1939
117 minutes   black and white   sound

Based on the poem by *Rudyard Kipling*
Adaptation, *Ben Hecht* and *Charles MacArthur*
Screenplay, *Joel Sayre, Fred Guiol*
Producer and director, *George Stevens*

CAST

Cutter, *Cary Grant*; MacChesney, *Victor McLaglen*; Ballantine, *Douglas Fairbanks, Jr.*; Gunga Din, *Sam Jaffe*; Gura, *Eduardo Ciannelli*; Emmy, *Joan Fontaine*; Colonel Weed, *Montagu Love*; Higginbotham, *Robert Coote*

OF MICE AND MEN

United Artists   1939
107 minutes   black and white   sound

Based on the novel by *John Steinbeck*
Screenplay, *Eugene Solow*
Director and producer, *Lewis Milestone*

CAST

George, *Burgess Meredith*; Mae, *Betty Field*; Lennie, *Lon Chaney, Jr.*; Slim, *Charles Bickford*; Candy, *Roman Bohnen*; Curley, *Bob Steele*; Whit, *Noah Beery, Jr.*

ACADEMY AWARDS NOMINATION: best picture

THE PRIVATE LIVES OF ELIZABETH AND ESSEX

Warner Brothers–First National   1939
106 minutes   Technicolor   sound

Based on the play by *Maxwell Anderson*
Screenplay, *Norman Reilly Raine* and *Aeneas MacKenzie*
Director, *Michael Curtiz*
Producer, *Hal B. Wallis*

CAST

Queen Elizabeth, *Bette Davis*; Earl of Essex, *Errol Flynn*; Lady Penelope Gray, *Olivia de Havilland*; Francis Bacon, *Donald Crisp*; Earl of Tyrone, *Alan Hale*; Sir Walter Raleigh, *Vincent Price*

WUTHERING HEIGHTS

United Artists   1939
103 minutes   black and white   sound

From the novel by *Emily Brontë*
Screenplay, *Ben Hecht* and *Charles MacArthur*
Director, *William Wyler*
Producer, *Samuel Goldwyn*

CAST

Cathy, *Merle Oberon*; Heathcliffe, *Laurence Olivier*; Edgar, *David Niven*; Dr. Kenneth, *Donald Crisp*; Nellie, *Flora Robson*; Hindley, *Hugh Williams*; Isabella, *Geraldine Fitzgerald*; Mr. Earnshaw, *Cecil Kellaway*; Joseph, *Leo G. Carroll*

ACADEMY AWARDS: best black-and-white cinematography, *Gregg Toland*